By Any Other Name
It's Still Sex

11/04

Minister Kris,

It is such a sweet smelling savor in the nostrils of God. You. You character is the best!

Love,

Pastor B

By Any Other Name
It's Still Sex

Barbara Wallace Erkins
Foreword by James E. Blue

Dawn Treader Publications
He who treads the dawn is the Bright and Shining Morning Star™

A Ministry of
Morning Star And Company, Inc.
Detroit, Pittsburgh, Cleveland

By Any Other Name It's Still Sex
Published by
Dawn Treader Publications
2002

For Information
Morning Star And Company, Inc.
PO Box 22175
Beachwood, OH 44118

LIBRARY OF CONGRESS CATALOGING-IN-PUBLICATION DATA

Erkins, Barbara Wallace, 1950-
  By any other name it's still sex / Barbara Wallace Erkins; foreword by James E. Blue.
    p. cm.
Includes bibliographical references and index.
  ISBN 1-58993-025-8 (alk. paper)
  1. Sex--Religious aspects--Christianity. 2. Sexual ethics. I. Title.

BT708.E74 2002
241'.66--dc21

2002012659

Printed in the United States of America
02 03 04 05 06 07 08 — 10 9 8 7 6 5 4 3 2 1 0

To my three "Fathers"

Acknowledgements

To my Heavenly Father who has loved me forever and has been so gracious to release this revelation to me. There are no words for me to say, "I simply stand in awe of You ... thank you."

To my earthly Father, Charles E. Wallace, who through his marriage to his wife, my mother, Selma E. Wallace, beget me as the firstborn of their union. I thank him for believing I would one day write a book, even though he will never get to see it. (He passed away July 3, 1999.)

To my spiritual Father, who has imparted to me so much "life" through his allowing me to be aligned with his tremendous apostolic/prophetic anointing. It is that anointing that has birthed this book in me. "Dad, you will never know just how much I love you and Sister Pastor. I will never be the same."

To Kim-Andrea Belle Richardson, the one who was more influential in encouraging me to write than anyone else on earth. To the first one who read my first scrawled out, handwritten pages and said, "Pastor Barbara, you've got to write this book. It's inside you and you've got to get it out." to the one who orchestrated each and every detail in this publishing process. To the one who, aside from the Lord, made it all happen. Thanks a million, Kim!

To Rabbi Robert Daniels, who introduced to me, unbeknown to him, the "seed" for this book during my attendance to "A Taste of Judaism." Thanks Rabbi Daniels for an amazing experience.

To Pastor James E. Blue, Jr., a man of God who came into my life at the right time and said critical words yesterday, that still impact my life today. Pastor Blue, you pastored me in the early days when solid foundational truths mattered most, thank God for you.

To Dr. Patricia T. Whitelocke, an anointed woman of God, who through her awesome teaching of God's Word would cause me to sit on the edge of my seat, as tears streamed down my face and met under my chin. You are still the greatest inspiration to me of women in ministry. You were one of the most instrumental in getting me headed in the right direction. Thanks.

To M. Ruth, it doesn't matter so much to me that you are a sage in the Body of Christ, but that you have for so many, many years been a sage to me! From the moment God directed my path to you, until this very day it has been your timely words of Godly wisdom that is still transforming my life. You're the best!! I love you.

To Lane, you have been with me through a zillion of my ups and downs and always kept me laughing. I love you, Lane. Thanks for being my friend.

To Deacons James and Barb, it was your commitment to me in my early walk of a "new single lifestyle," that has carved a special spot in my heart of you forever. You both were such an anchor for me and the first ones to teach me to be accountable, I love you. Thanks.

Thanks to Pastor Rita Wiley, Pastor Gayle Newmann, Pastor Veronica Hamilton, Dr. and Mrs. John and Camille Erkins, Marita Pompeani, The Eagles' Vision Christian Center family, all the reviewers, all the proof-readers, and editors.

To my children, Justin, I appreciate your critique of my writing early on, when I was only a third of the way through, and yet you said it was a precipitous to re-think many aspects of your young adult life. Jessica, I still remember the night you came into the living room with tears streaming down your face and said you were thankful to God for my book, because it confirmed many things the Lord was already speaking to your heart. Both of you have been such an inspiration to me, love you bunches.

To my husband, Jesse, your quiet supportive way of encouraging me to write has meant everything to me. I am so glad you kept saying, "Babe, keep writing." I am a very blessed wife to have a husband like you, I love you.

Contents

SEXUALITY IS AN INTEGRAL part of our lives. For many it forms the basis for self-identification and worth, and for others it is an undefined mystery. Sex has been categorized as unmentionable yet unavoidable. As popular as it is today, to discuss it in any detail remains taboo.

We cannot afford to ignore, hide, or fantasize about sex anymore. To do so could be lethal to not only our physical being, but to our emotional, psychological, and spiritual health. There is an epidemic in our nation regarding sexual problems. Venereal disease is no longer just an "adult" problem, and AIDS has ravaged the land. Pastor Barbara has written an intriguing and thought-provoking book that will challenge where you stand on the sex issue.

Yes, sex is an issue, and, it is not just an issue for Christians, but for everyone. Sexual problems are not exclusive to any one group. They affect all of us. *By Any Other Name It's Still Sex* challenges us to look not only at how we view sex, but to examine our own sexuality.

Without shame and in intriguing and often humorous fashion, Pastor Barbara brings us face to face with the sex issue. In examining the scriptures, she shares one dimension of what is going on and where we have failed.

By Any Other Name It's Still Sex paints a picture of how it all began. In the intimate setting of man's first encounter with God, was it an apple that caused the fall? What did we lose in the garden, what did we inherit from it, can we ever undo the damage? Pastor

Barbara gives us not only answers but hope.

James E. Blue

Introduction

I TAKE GREAT PLEASURE in that the Lord has allowed me to write this book at this time in my life. Now when I say *great pleasure*, I truly mean great pleasure! Do you have any idea how many times in the past I tried to write? No, you can't possibly imagine. I will not even begin to tax you with that story. All I can say is I have tried many times to write; but could never pull my thoughts and concepts together, but on this round the Lord has helped me tremendously.

As a matter of fact, in 1995 my dad gave me $1,700.00 seed money to write my would be first book. Well, needless to say (but I'll say it anyway), that ended up being used for a totally shot transmission in our 1983 Volvo wagon—such is life! We read in scripture that Abraham rejoiced to see the revelation of Christ in his day, even though he did not see the flesh and blood Son of God. Well, likewise, my dad will not only rejoice to see this book in his day, at the ripe old age of 81 years,* but he will probably get a monumental thrill out of being able to actually hold onto something that will connect him with that $1,700.00 he thinks I probably allowed someone, certainly not me, to squander on riotous living (smile).

As I take pen in hand, I am somewhat apprehensive and have a myriad of emotions with regard to the content, simply because it will dispel and cancel so much misunderstood theology. However, if we all take a deep breath, fasten our seat belts, and count to ten slowly, we will find the journey will be pretty exciting and will hopefully leave you with a never before eye-opening experience.

Pastor Barbara Wallace Erkins 1999

*My dad passed away on July 3, 1999. He did not see the finished project.

The Walk Of Integrity

I HEARD FROM A reliable source, a minister of the gospel who shall remain anonymous, that a most shocking comment was made not long ago, which reflects an attitude many males have about women in the church. A young man supposedly ran into one of his friends at a nightclub one Saturday night. A club the young people frequent in a particular city. These guys were talking and sharing as they looked around at the women, and just then, an attractive female walked pass. The friend quickly informed his buddy that she attended such and such a church and "they've (this particular church) got the baddest 'ho's (whores) in town at that church." With great delight, the friend received this very exciting news and promptly made a mental note to attend this particular mega-church to see if this was true. He not only found that the attractive beauties were definitely there, but he was also able to get one of the exciting "little numbers" in the bed with absolutely no problem at all. The young man, after his one night encounter, later told his friend that this easy score really was a disappointment to him, especially since she was supposed to be a "Christian." This is the kind of thing that is so very sad for the church. It is also a well-known fact among the guys out in the streets that getting a woman in the church is a "good piece of _ _ _," because she has been "saving herself." God help us all!

Part One

I disapprove of what you say,
but I will defend to the death your right to say it.
— Voltaire

Those Crazy Days Back When

Now in the sixth month the angel Gabriel was sent by God to a city of Galilee named Nazareth, to a virgin betrothed to a man whose name was Joseph, of the house of David. The virgin's name was Mary. And having come in, the angel said to her, "Rejoice, highly favored one, the Lord is with you; blessed are you among women!" But when she saw him, she was troubled at his saying, and considered what manner of greeting this was. Then the angel said to her, "Do not be afraid, Mary, for you have found favor with God. And behold, you will conceive in your womb and bring forth a Son, and shall call His name JESUS. He will be great, and will be called the Son of the Highest; and the Lord God will give Him the throne of His father David. And He will reign over the house of Jacob forever, and of His kingdom there will be no end." Then Mary said to the angel, "How can this be, since I do not know a man?" And the angel answered and said to her, "The Holy Spirit will come upon you, and the power of the Highest will overshadow you; therefore, also, that Holy One who is to be born will be called the Son of God. Now indeed, Elizabeth your relative has also conceived a son in her old age; and this is now the sixth month for her who was called barren. For with God nothing will be impossible." Then Mary said, "Behold the maidservant of the Lord! Let it be to me according to your word." And the angel departed from her.—Luke 1:26-38

I have always found it fascinating, haven't you, that God would find this young, single, virgin woman and impregnate her with His Son? I mean think about it ladies, (sorry men, but females are the only ones who can relate here), how many of you remember when a young lady was single and had committed the "BIG SIN" before God, the sheer terror she would face? Now mind you, no one is ever aware of what she has done until she starts to look like she swallowed a *'watermelon whole'*. Then her every thought would be about the church, the community, her favorite teacher, and God forbid, the pastor and her parents. All these people would fast forward through the fallen's mind like an electronic Rolodex. She would be so terrified of what to do, and most of all, what they would now think of her. As far as she was concerned, this was nothing short of a lose-lose situation, because in the African-American community all daughters were told, "don't come to my door with a package and no husband!" This statement was usually made only one time, and those parents meant it. Hence, their daughter, their "precious wonder", would sit around with one horrible vision after another about her funeral. She figured, "surely my parents are going to kill me, so I might as well prepare to meet my Maker" (smile).

Then there were the more innovative parents (schemers are what they really were) whose daughters would have these "*I MUST MARRY HIM IN MY PARENTS LIVING ROOM TODAY BECAUSE I LOVE HIM SO MUCH RIGHT NOW OR DIE*" weddings. These wedding arrangements would come together so fast; they would have family and neighbors' heads spinning! We didn't know folks could move so fast!

The others I remember most are the girls who resorted to wearing their very heavy plaid "carcoats" (that's what we called them in the 60's) right up until those last couple of weeks of school. We are talking the month of June, here, O.K.? We were in school until the middle of the month in those days. We are talking hot, humid, muggy, sticky Cincinnati, Ohio weather. As we questioned and probed them about what was up with the heavy carcoat, they would vow to you over and over again that they had been experiencing a chilly feeling for months and months and just could not get warm to save their lives. I would tend to agree. It was probably the fear of the cold chill of death they knew was certain if their Momma ever reached out and grabbed that girl by the throat because of what she had done! As we would stroll home from school together, the "much touched" (the ones whose boyfriends had scored the big move), and the "untouched" (those of us who went no further than heavy, heavy, heavy petting; we still felt kind of saintly you know) would be looking at the much touched and wondering if they were going to finally pass out from total heat exhaustion, or collapse under the heavy load of books (time for final exams) they were carrying to conceal that fast swelling mid-section of theirs, hidden under those hot carcoats.

The last group was your praying group. These were the ones who were banging and grumbling at the door of God's throne room morning, noon, and night. Their constant prayer was a cry for Him to awaken them out of their nightmare, because after all this cannot be real! "How could this happen to me?," they quizzically wanted to know. Based on my 12th grade health class marriage unit, I knew how it had happened and I wanted to tell them. That was that little Miss-know-it-all side of me attempting to emerge. I, however, never said a mumbling word. In the marriage unit, back in "my day," they used to teach you about what to expect on the wedding night. I really thought all the girls in the class, looking around half shocked, were really as shocked as some of us virgins who were ruby red from all our blushing. Then a few months after graduation, I found out many of them had already had their wedding night experience long before we had the marriage unit in the health class. I guess they were trying to throw the naïve group off their trail.

Well, back to the praying group. We know God is a God that hears and answers prayers; therefore, some of them would get their wish, and would miraculously start their monthly cycle. It would spontaneously show up out of nowhere. Believe me, it was only a rare few that experienced that miracle. Most of them, however, had to go the way of those brave souls that had blazed the deeply gouged out trail before them. I even remember hearing about a young lady who tried to convince her mother that her pregnancy happened the same as Mary, the mother of Jesus—let's all say "NOT"!

We all understand, at some level, the trauma young people

must experience when there is a pregnancy out of wedlock. Even today in this 21st century hip-hop generation, this issue still creates quite a stir in the life of a young teen and her family (you notice I didn't say, "a young teen and HIS family"). Many families still find the out-of-wedlock pregnancy so hard to handle. Hence, abortion is so prevalent.

In Luke 1:34, Mary plainly states that she has not *known* a man. There is still so much that is secret and hidden from human beings who have not known one another from a sexual perspective. Something happens, a true dynamic occurs in the spirit realm when one learns of and knows someone sexually. God, in His infinite wisdom, knew Mary was paying a very high price to consent to His request. He wanted her and Joseph to know, however, without a doubt that the "sexual knowing" of each other was something He did not want them to experience before Jesus was both conceived and birthed into this world. Why was that so important to God? I wonder, don't you?

IT FEELS GOOD NOT TO KNOW

YOU KNOW, BEING A product of the 50's and 60's certainly positions me to have a wide range of thought regarding human sexuality and how I have witnessed its evolution over the decades. After all, I was born in an era when there was still a tendency toward a more demure, somewhat Victorian attitude regarding sex. It was an attitude as well as a spirit over our nation at large. It's amazing how that Victorian cloud was still hanging over our nation during the "baby boomer" years, when all those babies were born post W.W.II! Today, however, we have a full-blown sexual explosion on our hands, birthed with the discovery of the pill.

While acting chaste is certainly worlds apart from being chaste, it is still not an impossible state of existence. Being chaste was not impossible during the time Jesus Christ walked the earth (my kids call it "the olden days"), but it is not impossible now. As a matter of fact, I will venture to say God is still looking for a few good men and women who will do as Jesus Christ, His Son, did and walk pure before Him.

In looking at the life of Jesus Christ we find that our sinless, spotless, Savior of this sin-cursed world never "knew" a woman. Jesus purposed to point this out to His disciples. In Luke 9:58 we read, "And Jesus said to him, 'Foxes have holes and birds of the air have nests, but the Son of Man has nowhere to lay His head.'"

In understanding what is sometimes referred to as an orientalism (a saying, proverb, parable or story of an eastern culture), we in this western civilization have greatly misunderstood what Jesus was saying. He was not making this statement as a vow of poverty, which many of us have customarily believed. He was saying this to make it very clear to all of His would be disciples, "Hey boys, I'm single, I'm free, I am not married and don't have to answer to a soul. I am simply here to do my Father's will." Now I ask you, when does a fox go to find a hole, when does a bird prepare to build a nest? When it is time to procreate, that's when! When it is time to mate. These animals are with their families of origin until it is time for them to start the mating process themselves. Only at this point do they leave their family of origin to begin their own families. Another point to keep in mind regarding Jesus' statement, within the context of this passage is the disciples' response. The disciples had too many pressing issues to handle (verses 59-62). Jesus truly understood the freedom he had a single male to stay focused and travel full steam ahead. No looking back, no extraneous family affairs to attend to, no looking at the distractions on his right hand and on his left. He had a clear focus and was on a mission simply to advance his father's kingdom.

Now let's back up a little and take a look at John the Baptist. He is the forerunner for Christ, the Savior of the world. John makes an important declaration in Luke 3:4-6:

> As it is written in the book of the words of Isaiah the prophet, saying: "The voice of one crying in the wilderness: 'Prepare the way of the LORD, Make His paths straight. Every valley shall be filled and every mountain and hill brought low; the crooked places shall be made straight and the rough ways smooth; and all flesh shall see the salvation of God.'"

During his brief ministry on earth, we know he was not only raised by his parents according to the vow of the Nazarite, Luke 1:15 and Numbers 6:2-5; but it has also been historically documented that he studied with a group called the Essenes.

The Essenes

"[The community of Essenes] was strictly organized as

a single body at the head of which were presidents to whom the members were bound in unconditional obedience. One wishing to enter the order received three badges – a pickax, an apron, and a white garment. After a year's probation, he was admitted to the purification ceremonies. Another probation of two years followed, after which he was allowed to participate in the common meals and to become a full member. At that time, the new member took a fearful oath in which he bound himself to absolute openness to his brethren and secrecy concerning the doctrines of the order to nonmembers. Only adults were admitted as members, but children were received for instruction in the principles of Essenism. Josephus says that the Essenes were divided into four classes according to the time of their entrance, the children being the first class, those in the two stages of the novitiate the second and third class, and the members proper the fourth class.

[Concerning their ethics, manners, and customs] Philo competes with Josephus in sounding the praises of the Essenes. According to these authorities, their life was moderate, simple, and unpretentious. They condemned sensual desires as sinful and abstained from wedlock but chose other people's children while they were pliable and fit for learning. They took food and drink only [until] they had had enough, contenting themselves with the same dish day by day and rejecting great expense as harmful to mind and body. They did not cast away clothes and shoes until they were utterly useless and sought to acquire only what was needed for the wants of life." [1]

So here we have both the Savior of the World, Jesus Christ, and John the Baptist, His forerunner, never having experienced those normal "boy plus girl" encounters, and they both attended unto God without distraction.

Folks I ask you, have you found sex to be a pretty big distraction for you? I have. God has placed in the scriptures some key information He wants His children to understand with regard to this whole issue of sex. His thoughts and feelings are very important and He wants us to know how He truly feels about it. He especially wants it known to His church family.

Have you ever stopped to think about how easy we can conquer those distractions? We can do it when we fast and pray. Some of you are asking what does fasting have to do with sex. Let's read what the Bible says in 1 Corinthians 7:5:

> *Do not deprive one another except with consent for a time, that you may give yourselves to fasting and prayer; and come together again so that satan does not tempt you because of your lack of self-control.*

This really started me wondering about Jesus in the wilderness for forty days and forty nights, or Moses away from his wife and up in the mountain with God for forty days and forty nights. We have John, don't forget, in the wilderness wearing camel's hair and eating locusts and honey. I'm sure that was where he spent a great portion of his time, off somewhere alone with God when he was not ministering repentance to man. So here we have one man, Jesus, who was single and pulled away to be alone with God; the other man was married, Moses, but he too pulled away to be alone with God. The third man, John, simply served God in the faithful simplicity of his single lifestyle. There is certainly a well-orchestrated plan by God in having His people sacrifice themselves in this way.

A Serious 'Dear John' Letter

I also want to note that John had no greater persecution come against him in his life than when Herod became infuriated over John's public denouncement of Herod's illicit relationship with his sister-in-law, Herodias. We read in Luke 3:19-20:

> *But Herod the tetrarch, being rebuked by him concerning Herodias, his brother Philip's wife, and for all the evils which Herod had done, also added this, above all, that he shut John up in prison.*

This situation resulted in John's imprisonment. To add insult to injury, it was an extremely explicit dance by Herodias' daughter, Salome, that so titillated Herod that he vowed to give up to half of his kingdom to Salome. All she had to do was name her price. She did. At her mother's request, she asked Herod for the head of John the Baptist on a charger! Mark 6:14-29 says:

> *Now King Herod heard of Him, for His name had become well known. And he said, "John the Baptist is risen from the dead, and therefore these powers are at work in him." Others said, "It is Elijah." And others said, "It is the Prophet, or like one of the prophets." But when Herod heard, he said, "This is John, whom I beheaded; he has been raised from the dead!" For Herod himself had sent and laid hold of John, and bound him in prison for the sake of Herodias, his brother Philip's wife; for he had married her. For John had said to Herod, "It is not lawful for you to have your brother's wife." Therefore Herodias held it against him and wanted to kill him, but she could not; for Herod feared John, knowing that he was a just and holy man, and he protected him. And when he heard him, he did many things, and heard him gladly. Then an opportune day came when Herod on his birthday gave a feast for his nobles, the high officers, and the chief men of Galilee. And when Herodias' daughter herself came in and danced, and pleased Herod and those who sat with him, the king said to the girl, "Ask me whatever you want, and I will give it to you." He also swore to her, "Whatever you ask me, I will give you, up to half of my kingdom." So she went out and said to her mother, "What shall I ask?" And she said, "The head of John the Baptist!" Immediately she came in with haste to the king and asked, saying, "I want you to give me at once the head of John the Baptist on a platter." And the king was exceedingly sorry; yet, because of the oaths and because of those who sat with him, he did not want to refuse her. Immediately the king sent an executioner and commanded his head to be brought. And he went and beheaded him in prison, brought his head on a platter, and gave it to the girl; and the girl gave it to her mother. When his disciples heard of it, they came and took away his corpse and laid it in a tomb.*

Clearly, we see how satan directly opposed John for speaking out with righteous indignation against this illicit affair, which totally opposed the laws of God with regard to sex and marriage. Then to totally mock the whole situation, satan turned right around and by his own perverted means used sexual stimulation, as Salome danced, to so lure Herod into an irrational state of mind that sex ultimately became the tool used which resulted in John's death! This forerunner of Christ, who knew no sexual sin at all, was killed because of the very power of the same. Yes, we know that John had to decrease so that Christ would increase (John 3:30); but who was used and how they did it will be judged by God!

Do we truly realize how much the enemy has used sex to bring our world into the totally corrupt state it is in today? Now we will not be remiss in taking responsibility for giving him a whole lotta' help; we have indeed! We cannot, however, blame it all on the devil. Amen. Our society is so preoccupied with this three-letter word, S-E-X, it would boggle the mind to stop and think about how much damage it truly does on earth! With as much pleasure as it brings on the one hand, on the other hand when it is misused and out of control, it is nothing more than a weapon of destruction.

Now that we have taken a brief look at the lives of Jesus Christ and John the Baptist and their "NO SEX" policy, let's look back in time where the origin of all things began. As we do this, we will get clear insight into foundational truths we must understand and a real handle on the purpose of this book.

A Smorgasbord Fill-up

THEN GOD SAID, "LET Us make man in Our image, according to Our likeness; let them have dominion over the fish of the sea, over the birds of the air, and over the cattle, over all the earth and over every creeping thing that creeps on the earth." So God created man in His own image; in the image of God He created him; male and female He created them. Then God blessed them, and God said to them, "Be fruitful and multiply; fill the earth and subdue it; have dominion over the fish of the sea, over the birds of the air, and over every living thing that moves on the earth." And God said, "See, I have given you every herb that yields seed which is on the face of all the earth, and every tree whose fruit yields seed; to you it shall be for food. Also, to every beast of the earth, to every bird of the air, and to everything that creeps on the earth, in which there is life, I have given every green herb for food"; and it was so. Then God saw everything that He had made, and indeed it was very good. So the evening and the morning were the sixth day.

Thus the heavens and the earth, and all the host of them, were finished. And on the seventh day God ended His work which He had done, and He rested on the seventh day from all His work which He had done. Then God blessed the seventh day and sanctified it, because in it He rested from all His work which God had created and made.

This is the history of the heavens and the earth when they were created, in the day that the LORD God made the earth and the heavens, before any plant of the field was in the earth and before any herb of the field had grown. For the LORD God had not caused it to rain on the earth, and there was no man to till the ground; but a mist went up from the earth and watered the whole face of the ground. And the LORD God formed man of the dust of the ground, and breathed into his nostrils the breath of life; and man became a living being.

The LORD God planted a garden eastward in Eden, and there He put the man whom He had formed. And out of the ground the LORD God made every tree grow that is pleasant to the sight and good for food. The tree of life was also in the midst of the garden, and the tree of the knowledge of good and evil… Then the LORD God took the man and put him in the garden of Eden to tend and keep it. And the LORD God commanded the man, saying, "Of every tree of the garden you may freely eat; but of the tree of the knowledge of good and evil you shall not eat, for in the day that you eat of it you shall surely die."

And the LORD God said, "It is not good that man should be alone; I will make him a helper comparable to him." Out of the ground the LORD God formed every beast of the field and every bird of the air, and brought them to Adam to see what he would call them. And whatever Adam called each living creature, that was its name. So Adam gave names to all cattle, to the birds of the air, and to every beast of the field. But for Adam there was not found a helper comparable to him. And the LORD God caused a deep sleep to fall on Adam, and he slept; and He took one of his ribs, and closed up the flesh in its place. Then the rib which the LORD God had taken from man He made into a woman, and He brought her to the man. And Adam said: "This is now bone of my bones And flesh of my flesh; she shall be called Woman, because she was taken out of Man."

Therefore a man shall leave his father and mother and be joined to his wife, and they shall become one flesh. And they were both naked, the man and his wife, and were not ashamed.

Now the serpent was more cunning than any beast of the field which the LORD God had made. And he said to the woman, "Has God indeed said, 'You shall not eat of every tree of the garden'?" And the woman said to the serpent, "We may eat the fruit of the trees of the garden; but of the fruit of the tree which is in the midst of the garden, God has said, 'You shall not eat it, nor shall you touch it, lest you die.' " Then the serpent said to the woman, "You will not surely die. For God knows that in the day you eat of it your eyes will be opened, and you will be like God, knowing good and evil." So when the woman saw that the tree was good for food, that it was pleasant to the eyes, and a tree desirable to make one wise, she took of its fruit and ate. She also gave to her husband with her, and he ate. Then the eyes of both of them were opened, and they knew that they were naked; and they sewed fig leaves together and made themselves coverings. And they heard the sound of the LORD God walking in the garden in the cool of the day, and Adam and his wife hid themselves from the presence of the LORD God among the trees of the garden.

Then the LORD God called to Adam and said to him, "Where are you?" So he said, "I heard Your voice in the garden, and I was afraid because I was naked; and I hid myself." And He said, "Who told you that you were naked? Have you eaten from the tree of which I commanded you that you should not eat?" Then the man said, "The woman whom You gave to be with me, she gave me of the tree, and I ate." And the LORD God said to the woman, "What is this you have done?" The woman said, "The serpent deceived me, and I ate." So the LORD God said to the serpent: "Because you have done this, you are cursed more than all cattle, and more than every beast of the field; on your belly you shall go, and you shall eat dust all the days of your life. And I will put enmity between you and the woman, and between your seed and her Seed; He shall bruise your head, and you shall bruise His heel." Genesis 1:26—3:15

For the longest we have wrestled with trying to get an understanding as to what in the world could Adam and Eve have been thinking about while in the Garden. They blew it for all mankind--forever! After all, did they really lose their minds or what? I want to make a quick detour right here and say this long standing myth about the fruit they ate from the tree, the proverbial apple, is total error. To all who have labored under this misconception forever, go back, re-read the scriptures, and look for the "apple" word. When you find it, give me a call (smile).

Please note for those reading this book that I have taken into consideration the fact that my reader may not have a grasp of the Olde' King's English terminology and God's metaphorical way of speaking. It is this writer's intention to convey her revelations and ideas in such a way as to cause as little confusion about concepts as possible.

If we look at Genesis 2:17, we see a direct command by God not to eat of the tree of the knowledge of good and evil. Now, let's take for instance a common tree that grows in America—the Oak. O.K. Oak is the name of the tree and the acorn is its fruit. Pear trees produce pears, apple trees, apples, and so on. The name of the tree that God instructed them about was KNOWLEDGE. The fruit this tree produced was not the typical one fruit, but two. One fruit was called GOOD and the other fruit was called EVIL. In this case, when God speaks in terms of eating, He is speaking spiritually and not literally. Let's look at other scriptures:

Your words were found, and I ate them. Jeremiah 15:16

Moreover He said to me, "Son of man, eat what you find; eat this scroll, and go, speak to the house of Israel." Ezekiel 3:1

The *Strong's Concordance* reference number for eat in Genesis 2:17 is the same as for Jeremiah 15:16 and Ezekiel 3:1, and that is to consume or devour.

But He said to them, "I have food to eat of which you do not know." Therefore the disciples said to one another, "Has anyone brought Him anything to eat?" Jesus said to them, "My food is to do the will of Him who sent Me, and to finish His work." John 4:32-34

God was saying don't take "into the mind," don't allow your mind to be consumed with the good or the evil knowledge from this tree. If you devour, consume, refresh yourselves with this fruit it will be too hot to handle. It will kill you!

Stop and think about this. How many times have you made comments like, "Oh! That book was so good, I devoured it in a matter of days!"? Perhaps you said something like, "The presentation was excellent, and I ate every word they said." We speak of taking information into our minds as if we have eaten it. What Adam and Eve ate was the lie of satan! What satan had to say was heard with very hungry ears. They believed it, took it into their spirits and their hearts, thereby consuming every morsel of his fruit. They consumed, devoured, and refreshed themselves (so they thought) with his lie.

This tree in the garden was unique in that it produced two fruits. It was a tree of all knowledge, the tree of the Omniscient God. All knowledge belongs to and is owned by God, whether good or evil. I am sure it feels a bit taboo to say that God has any ownership over that which is evil, but I believe He does. All things were made by Him and without Him there was not anything made that was made. (John 1:3). Knowledge is a thing, it is ethereal, but it is a thing, nevertheless. God had to know what evil was; in its most basic form in order to know there was a need to protect Adam and Eve from it. It would have been totally contrary to the nature of God, Himself, to put all good around His created beings. He is a God that always seems to present both sides of the package, and allows us the freedom to choose.

This tree of knowledge had fruit that was good—Godly truths and principles that brought forth life; but it also produced fruit that was evil—satan's lies and deceptive tactics that brought destruction. By the mere fact that Adam and Eve disobeyed God by the very act of eating of the tree they were commanded not to eat of, guess what fruit they ate—right, evil!

Whenever we disobey God, we are partaking of the schemes and plans of the enemy whether we know it or not. Now this lie is two-fold; not only did they eat satan's information, but they also acted on the information. We humans may not plan on a conscious level to act on negative information when we hear it, but on some level, we always do. We either discard it as soon as we get it, or we ponder it and follow those little promptings that come up on the inside of us after we have digested and had our fill, which usually gets us into major trouble. The Bible says in Romans 3:4b, " . . . Indeed, let God be true but every man a liar".

We are not just liars because we do not speak the truth; we

are also liars because we do not do the truth! The Bible says in James 1:22, "But be doers of the word, and not hearers only, deceiving yourselves".

For every single piece of information we feed to our minds, whether a lie or the truth, we eat, consume, and take it in with the plan to either directly or indirectly act on it. We will become doers of the truth or doers of a lie. Therefore, Adam and Eve did not just hear satan tell them a lie and listen, but they believed the lie so much so they made a choice to act on it, too! The big question is what did they do? I am glad you asked that question. Hold onto your seatbelts . . . they had SEX! The fruit they ate, consumed, devoured, and refreshed themselves with was sex!

I would like to go on record here and say that there is so much revelation that God's people are now accessing on a regular basis, until it behooves all of us to maintain a framework of openness and teachableness. We are learning more and more about the Bible as revelation is being unveiled. It is this writer's intention to keep an open mind with regard to new insights and revelation that is yet to be made known. We therefore can safely conclude that the revelation about the sexual sin is not necessarily the end all and be all to what happened in the Garden of Eden. Who can know the mind of God? I would say it was, however, perhaps the greatest contributing factor to the infraction that occurred by Adam and Eve. Well Barbara, how in the world did you come to this conclusion? Are you really saying Adam and Eve had sex and that it contributed to the sinful act?

Let The Punishment Fit The Crime

*I*N OUR SOCIETY WE have the notion that somehow the punishment should fit the crime. God is also an advocate of the same. In Old Testament scripture we read in Exodus 21:23 – 25:

> *But if any harm follows, then you shall give life for life, eye for eye, tooth for tooth, hand for hand, foot for foot, burn for burn, wound for wound, stripe for stripe.*

Whatever you did to someone, the same would be done in return to you. This is a case where the punishment fits the crime. In the Gospels Jesus says this in Matthew 5:29-30:

> *If your right eye causes you to sin, pluck it out and cast it from you; for it is more profitable for you that one of your members perish, than for your whole body to be cast into hell. And if your right hand causes you to sin, cut it off and cast it from you; for it is more profitable for you that one of your members perish, than for your whole body to be cast into hell.*

Even though none of us makes a practice of tearing body parts from our frame when these parts have participated in sinful deeds, we do understand Jesus was addressing a principle here. The principle being, "Declare the body part guilty as charged and punish the part and not the entire body."

In the New Testament we read: Ephesians 4:28:

> *Let him who stole steal no longer, but rather let him labor, working with his hands what is good, that he may have*

something to give him who has need.

In other words, allow these hands to be used to do what brings honor and not what brings disgrace.

If mom puts fresh baked cookies in the cookie jar under the watchful eyes of little Johnny and he begins to cry for one, but mom says he can't have one until after he has eaten his dinner, what's next? Little Johnny may not be able to resist the temptation to take one even though he knows it is in direct disobedience to his mom. When mom's back is turned, he reaches into the jar to get one, but before he can get it to his mouth for a quick taste test, mom is back in the kitchen and has caught him red-handed. As if on automatic pilot he releases the cookie from his hand that is now conveniently hidden behind his back and he lets it roll under the kitchen table. Too late. Mom goes to the kitchen drawer pulls out a wooden spoon and doles out a couple of licks in that same disobedient hand, after she manages to get it out from hiding. Why did Johnny, at his very young age, hide his little hand behind his back? He did it because it is instinctively in us to want to hide the instruments of wrongdoing, whatever they may be. Little Johnny's now throbbing hand will be a reminder the next time he is tempted to steal with that body part that ended up being punished.

If the husband or wife to Jane and Sam bursts into the bedroom and catches Jane and Sam committing adultery, the first thing Jane and Sam are going to do is scramble for a sheet, a blanket, or something to cover up those body parts that are engaging in the act of being sexually satisfied. Jane is not going to try to cover the hair on her head and Sam is not going to grab socks to put over his big toe. They will try to cover those body parts that have committed the sinful act that has brought immediate guilt and shame.

Now let's look at other body parts for example. If we are prone to listening to gossip, we try to make our ears behave. If our Achilles heel is telling one lie on top of another, on top of another, we make a strong attempt at taming that unruly tongue. Perhaps every time we turn around we have our hands on pornography and it appears that our eyes can't seem to get enough of it; so we have to really work overtime in making ourselves read wholesome books instead. In each of the above examples, it is punishment enough just to try to overcome these challenges if any or all of them serve to be a weakness for us. We all know how painful it is to stop doing what we really don't want to do in our heart, but as they say, "No pain, no gain!"

I, therefore, surmise that Adam and Eve would not be conversing with God about their knowledge of their nakedness, after they sinned, unless the naked body itself had been engaging in sex. I mean, come on now. Why would they be ashamed of being naked just because they listened to the enemy say something? Why is nakedness even an issue at all when they had always been naked? There is no rhyme or reason for any other conclusion other than what seems to be the natural progression.

Please continue to read with an open heart and mind. Remain teachable to allow the Lord to speak to your heart the things He wants you to know. By the way, let's not forget that the last two men who ushered us out from under the Old Testament/Old Covenant were Jesus Christ, the Son of God, and John the Baptist. It is critical that we understand this.

Part Two

I wish he would explain his explanation.
—*Lord Byron*

... But Everybody Does It

THE LAST TWO MAJOR players (Jesus Christ, the Son of God, and John the Baptist) before the birthing of the church on the day of Pentecost in the book of Acts, were men who had never, ever, had sexual intercourse, and had no sexual contacts of any kind.

Remember, it was their belief (Essenism) that sensual pleasures were served only to distract them from the worship of God. It was extremely crucial on their part not to have had any sexual involvement if this world were ever to be reconciled back to God.

By the way, what's up with that anyway? If sex is such a normal and wonderful thing that every "normal" human being is to experience, then why would God not allow His only begotten Son to have a wife? We all have to die at some point, but in Jesus' case, He would just die differently than the rest of us "normal" people and His "normal" wife. Why couldn't Jesus just be "normal" like all the rest of us and have a wife and still die on the cross to save this sin-cursed world from utter destruction? It was utterly impossible, that's why! Let me be very clear in emphasizing this point so you will understand. This entire world fell into sin in the Garden of Eden because Adam and Eve engaged in sexual intercourse. Adam and Eve bought the bill of goods satan sold them. At that very moment, they relinquished ownership rights, and satan now had sole ownership of this world because of their fall. The only way this now lost and dying world could be transferred back into the hands of God, which we know was accomplished through the Blood of the Lamb, was to make sure that the "SURETY" (Jesus Christ) who was being put up for the re-sale and title transfer had "NO SEX!" The following statement is a common theme to keep in mind as you read this book in its entirety:

∽

FOR EVERY ACT OF SIN OR UNRIGHTEOUSNESS DONE, IT MUST BE COUNTERED WITH AN ACT OF RIGHTEOUSNESS EQUAL TO OR GREATER THAN AND CONTRARY TO THE ACT OF SIN DONE, IN ORDER TO CANCEL ITS AUTHORITY. ∽

When this happens, a clear title deed of transfer can be placed back into the hands of the original owner. We know that Jesus Christ was the only offering found worthy to redeem us and put us back into right standing with God. We read in Revelation 5:1-14:

> And I saw in the right hand of Him who sat on the throne a scroll written inside and on the back, sealed with seven seals. Then I saw a strong angel proclaiming with a loud voice, "Who is worthy to open the scroll and to loose its seals?" And no one in heaven or on the earth or under the earth was able to open the scroll, or to look at it. So I wept much, because no one was found worthy to open and read the scroll, or to look at it. But one of the elders said to me, "Do not weep. Behold, the Lion of the tribe of Judah, the Root of David, has prevailed to open the scroll and to loose its seven seals." And I looked, and behold, in the midst of the throne and of the four living creatures, and in the midst of the elders, stood a Lamb as though it had been slain, having seven horns and seven eyes, which are the seven Spirits of God sent out into all the earth. Then He came and took the scroll out of the right hand of Him who sat on the throne.
> Now when He had taken the scroll, the four living creatures and the twenty-four elders fell down before the Lamb, each having a harp, and golden bowls full of incense, which are the prayers of the saints. And they sang a new song, saying:

*"You are worthy to take the scroll, and to open its seals;
for You were slain, and have redeemed us to God by Your blood
Out of every tribe and tongue and people and nation, and have
made us kings and priests to our God; and we shall reign on the
earth."*

*Then I looked, and I heard the voice of many angels
around the throne, the living creatures, and the elders; and
the number of them was ten thousand times ten thousand, and
thousands of thousands, saying with a loud voice: "Worthy is the
Lamb who was slain to receive power and riches and wisdom,
and strength and honor and glory and blessing!"*

*And every creature which is in heaven and on the earth
and under the earth and such as are in the sea, and all that are in
them, I heard saying: "Blessing and honor and glory and power
be to Him who sits on the throne, and to the Lamb, forever and
ever!"*

*Then the four living creatures said, "Amen!" and the
twenty-four elders fell down and worshiped Him who lives
forever and ever.*

Seeing Ain't Believing

Sex is an extremely powerful force. Sex was a catalyst for
the fall of the great Roman Empire. As we clearly stated, sexual
sin is the destructive force unleashed in the earth that is wreaking
havoc on millions of lives today. It is necessary for us to get a true
understanding of what happened many thousands of years ago in the
Garden of Eden; this is so we will further understand why this area
of sex is such a stronghold today. The Bible tells us that satan was
more cunning than any beast of the field that God had made (Genesis
3:1). It is here we both need to see and understand how he unfolded
this wicked plot. Remember that satan was Lucifer before the fall. He
was the anointed cherub over God's throne room. He was not only a
spiritual being that was glorious, but he was extremely powerful and
brilliant when he dwelled in heaven. Did he lose all of this when God

ousted him? I think not! Now it's pretty apparent to us that God has planted zillions of trees in the earth; so there were plenty of trees in the Garden of Eden from which Adam and Eve could partake. It is unfortunate that all mankind's destiny hinged on those two not messing with just one tree! One tree!

If you are like me and have ever allowed your mind to wander, you have tried, as I have to imagine what the tree must have looked like. What was so appealing about the tree? Was it greener than green and bigger than big? Maybe the tree was kind of mean like those talking trees that threw apples at Dorothy and Scarecrow in the movie *The Wizard of Oz*. In other words, why all this focus on a tree? Well, there are a couple of mysteries I believe God is unfolding with regard to the tree. These truths have been hidden in the scriptures all along. As God brings this revelation out, it helps us to begin to piece this puzzle together, by putting the focus where it needs to be. Keep in mind, we are in a garden full of trees . . . the operative words are garden and tree.

Psalm 1:3 says, "He shall be like a tree . . . ."

Who shall be like a tree? Man! He, man, is the tree God does not want touched! We have all read and quoted this scripture many times. We know God makes comparisons to mankind as trees. Some of the scriptures where we see this are Matthew 7:17-20, Psalm 52: 8a and Proverbs 15:4:

> *Even so, every good tree bears good fruit, but a bad tree bears bad fruit. A good tree cannot bear bad fruit, nor can a bad tree bear good fruit. Every tree that does not bear good fruit is cut down and thrown into the fire. Therefore by their fruits you will know them. Matthew 7:17-20*

> *But I am like a green olive tree in the house of God; Psalm 52:8a*

> *A wholesome tongue is a tree of life, Proverbs 15:4*

Another scripture that holds a mystery is in Songs of Solomon 4:12 and 5:1:

A garden enclosed
Is my sister, my spouse,
A spring shut up,
A fountain sealed.

I have come to my garden, my sister, my spouse;
I have gathered my myrrh with my spice;
I have eaten my honeycomb with my honey;
I have drunk my wine with my milk.

In these verses, we see the woman referred to as a garden. There has been much controversy over whether or not Songs of Solomon is in reference to Jesus Christ, the Bridegroom and His church, the Bride, or is it about true married love between Solomon and the Shulamite woman. I believe Songs of Solomon could literally be written about both. We will better understand this, as we get further into the book.

Remember, the devil is so cunning. He was cunning and crafty enough to have so much of the Christian and non-Christian world thinking there was an issue of an eaten apple in the Garden of Eden. He had us blind-sided while the truth remained hidden.

Now if we go back and look at Psalm 1:3 and Songs of Solomon 4:12 and 5:1, keeping these scriptures in mind as we read Genesis 3:1-7, you will get an entirely new perspective on this major act of high treason Adam and Eve committed against God.

I Hate Blind Dates

All along in the Garden, Adam and Eve had been happily worshipping and communing with God. Now we all want to know the answer to the $64,000 question . . . how long were they in the Garden of Eden before they blew it? I, for one, will be a most unhappy camper if I get to glory and find out they blew it only a week and a half into this thing (smile)! They were God's gift of glory to the earth. They had total and complete dominion over everything under their feet, flying over their heads, and swimming in the seas. Guess what, satan was envious to the max! He was so envious of what Almighty God had done that he had to find a way to destroy the beauty and holiness of it. After all, it was Lucifer, as the anointed covering cherub, who used to possess such spiritual authority before he committed treason against God, thereby, losing his status and position of rulership. So here comes satan to whisper in Eve's ear, "Hey, look at your partner; take a real good look at Adam; I mean really look at him; don't you want some of that fruit?" he must have asked. Eve repeated back to him what God said regarding His instruction to them concerning the tree. Then satan said, "Oh, that's just His way of keeping you from being wise like Him!" All of a sudden, she looked, then did a double take, and looked again. As she began to look at his sexual organs, with this new insight from the serpent, a hungry desire for him was birthed within her loins. The old serpent began to give her a startling revelation. Before she knew it, there were desires and feelings being released in her body that she had never experienced before. The devil's wisdom, according to the Bible, is earthly and sensual. God's desire was to shield and protect Adam and Eve from this wisdom because He knew it was destructive. As her eyes were opened for the first time, in areas she was previously blinded to, the scripture says, " . . . she saw it was good for food and pleasant to the eyes." What did he really show her? Did he show her orgasmic pleasures and sexual climaxes that would just blow her mind if she could have just a "little taste of that tree, a little taste of the fruit hanging on it?" The Bible even tells us in Psalm 34:8:

> *Oh, taste and see that the LORD is good; Blessed is the man who trusts in Him!*

"Eat of Me," God was saying. Don't take pleasure and delight in eating of that in which you cannot trust, in that which will cause you such major disappointment.

The only sweet and pleasurable moments Adam and Eve knew were the wonderful times they spent loving and worshipping their Father. They only knew Him and how to love Him, nothing more. From the beginning, they had not ever trusted in anything but God . . . now this. Let's look more closely at how this fall came.

In Genesis 3:7-9 we read:

> *Then the eyes of both of them were opened, and they knew that they were naked; and they sewed fig leaves together and made themselves coverings. And they heard the sound of the LORD God walking in the garden in the cool of the day, and Adam and his wife hid themselves from the presence of the LORD God among the trees of the garden. Then the LORD God called to Adam and said to him, "Where are you?"*

Now we can see from verse nine that God was aware that something drastic had happened. He proceeds to question them, "Where are you?" In this case, we need to look at what God did not ask. What God really wanted to know was, "Where have you been? Your spirits have ventured into territory that was unfamiliar to you and it was without Me? We three have always been together in our worship and fellowship, but I sense a strange presence has come in and interrupted what we have always shared." We read in Genesis 4:1 the following:

> *Now Adam knew Eve his wife, and she conceived and bore Cain, and said, "I have acquired a man from the LORD."*

We know that even though God asked Adam and Eve this question, He was already very much aware of what had happened. The three of them, God, Adam, and Eve had always shared such beautiful communion together. This was the way it had always been. The cunning and wicked serpent hated the three of them being in this sweet place of unity, so he was "hell-bent" on breaking it up! Based on the way Genesis 4:1 reads, we get the impression that Adam and Eve did not have a sexual relationship until after the fall in Genesis 3:7-8. That's absolutely right. The two of them did not have a relationship in which Adam knew Eve intimately until we get to Genesis 4:1. So what actually happened? There were THREE of them in the sexually perverted act of Genesis 3:7, "Then the eyes of both of them were opened . . .." It was Adam, Eve, and satan, NOT TWO! This was satan's long awaited and planned for moment to bring them into intimacy with him, so he could spiritually ejaculate his seed into them and destroy them forever! How else would the sin nature get into all mankind forever?! How would the seed of sin otherwise be deposited in mankind? Seed is always deposited through intercourse, through germination, through pollination, but not through conversation! God, alone, is the only one with the power to speak a creative word; that will manifest into tangible results. The Bible says in Proverbs 18:21 that the power of death and life is in the tongue. He has also given us, His children, the power to speak a creative word, but not satan! We read in Genesis 3:15 the following:

> And I will put enmity between you and the woman, and between your seed and her Seed; He shall bruise your head, and you shall bruise His heel.

We clearly see in this verse that God is speaking of the seed of satan that has now been deposited into them. God is making satan aware of the fact that Eve may have been far too consenting in allowing her curiosity to get the best of her, therefore yielding to his temptation. However, she will come to utterly despise the very seed that he has now deposited into her and Adam . . . she will despise it forever!

Slippery When Wet

The major purpose satan had in seducing Eve was to get to Adam. He was out to destroy this man, and he made Eve his key assistant in weakening him and drawing him into what satan had strategically planned, a "menage-a-trois!" This, therefore, was not the occasion when Adam knew Eve intimately. This is when Adam knew satan and satan knew Adam; when Eve knew satan and satan knew Eve! He baited Eve and lured her into his sex-trap, where she succumbed to his touch and she in turn lured Adam in with her. What the three of them did was the most sensual and base of all sexual pleasures and sin known to man. Every sexual perversion that would ever be experienced by mankind was released into them right then and there. It was beyond comprehension—totally unimaginable! What we are seeing and hearing about in this 21st century, with regard to totally depraved sexual encounters people are sanctioning, is NEW TO US, but old business to the enemy. Every sexual perversion known to man has been around since the three of them entered into this wicked deed!

So, the master of all salesmen scored big when he seduced her into tasting of his wares. As my girlfriend says, "He is the *sell the sizzle* king!" Eve was so far roped in on this one, with satan; she exercised absolutely no resistance to his enticements. In those fleeting moments it was no longer the God of creation, her adoring Heavenly Father that she wanted, but her appetites had finally peaked and were out of control! The process of what took place is spelled out clearly in the book of James 1:13-15:

> *Let no one say when he is tempted, "I am tempted by God"; for God cannot be tempted by evil, nor does He Himself tempt anyone. But each one is tempted when he is drawn away by his own desires and enticed. Then, when desire has conceived, it gives birth to sin; and sin, when it is full-grown, brings forth death.*

Believe you me, if satan was powerful enough to draw away a third of the heavenly host from the very presence of God, then his drawing Adam and Eve away was mere child's play! The fallen angels had no ability to compete with the power of the "former great and mighty Lucifer," so what in the world was "little ole' green Eve" going to do once she was within range of his wicked wiles and his firepower? The same way he attempted to usurp authority over Almighty God in heaven above, was the same way he intended to make his power move on earth below. In this, we must always consider ourselves without Christ in us, the hope of glory, (Colossians 1:27) no match, no match at all for satan and his wickedness! Remember he is satan, previously Lucifer, a high ranking angel in heaven . . . he was *super bad* and he was "all that" when God created him!

Well, the evil deed was done. They had taken their fill of one another. They, Adam and Eve, had now fulfilled the enemy's request . . . sinned against their God. This sin they committed gave them knowledge they never possessed before, and with this newly acquired knowledge came the shame. The shame that comes from knowing.

When Green Looks White

WHETHER YOU WERE A person that was a virgin, male or female, right up until your wedding night, or you were like me and millions of others caught up in being sexually involved outside the bonds of holy matrimony—running around doing "your thing," when it came to sex; if you did not marry and do it right, you probably threw caution and sanctity to the wind. Why? Once one has tasted of the fruit of sexual pleasure, for the most part, a dangerous animal on the inside of us springs to life. It's called ***knowing***.

Just think back. There is a natural greenness and naiveté in a virgin. It is there whether she is 14 or 40. The same applies to males. There is this untouched area that rests upon this person's being. There is also a freshness to them that is many times evidenced in their personality. Parents can have a young, virgin teen at home and the family may have a pretty natural, free and wholesome attitude in regard to their sexuality.

Many times in these settings the teen may feel quite at ease running around the house in her underwear. She may think nothing of the fact that her dad or her brothers may see her rapidly developing body in such limited attire. Why? It is because she has not been awakened to that knowledge; she has no ***knowing*** regarding the power she possesses as a sexual being. We would do well to instruct all of our teens and young adults along the lines of what Songs of Solomon 2:7 says:

> *I charge you, O daughters of Jerusalem,*
> *By the gazelles or by the does of the field,*
> *Do not stir up nor awaken love until it pleases.*

It is usually only in those cases where parents emphasize strongly that the teen should be robed when walking around the house, that some teens even bother to cover themselves up at all. The Bible says, " . . . to the pure all things are pure." (Titus 1:15a). We know that some young teens are naturally modest and would not be without cover-up, but some are not.

Not surprisingly, though, as soon as that teen girl has tasted of the fruits of sex, she becomes smart-mouthed, and gets this I-don't-have-to-listen-to-anything-you-parents-have-to-say-attitude. Yes, flippancy shows up and unpacks its bags where innocence used to dwell. Along with the attitudinal changes, many times comes a change in dress, the addition of make-up, not to mention the out and out rebellion in the home. Have we not all witnessed this to some extent, or have been the guilty culprit ourselves? There is no longer a respectful attitude when addressing the parents. Many times a girl's whole attitude toward her dad starts to become very testy. She, the "New Ms. Wisdom," only has ears to hear what "he" (the proverbial boyfriend, soul mate, "my man," or lover) has to say. No one else knows or understands anything at all; everyone her parent's age and older are now the idiots, let "New Ms. Wisdom" tell it. This behavior begins to surface because the enemy is seducing her to the dark side of the force. She doesn't realize she, too, is being duped like Eve, and is slowly being roped into tying herself to the soul of the new "beloved."

Naturally, as I write, I am speaking from my perspective as a female. I know there are similar experiences, many times, for males; but fortunately, because they are designed by God to naturally be "givers" (females are "receivers") they don't tend to buck up against parental authority the same as females do. The male is designed by God to be a natural born leader; therefore, his capacity to adjust to the influence of "another authority" (a female lover) in conjunction with keeping a right attitude toward parental authority is many times easier for him to handle. On some level, factoring in females' tendency toward being the far more emotional creature, perhaps has some affect on these kinds of situations as well. In everything, we know there is always an exception to the rule; so, I am by no means advocating this line of thinking to be hard and fast.

I want to emphasize here that there is no difference in a male being a natural born leader versus a female being a natural born leader. The leadership of "the home" from the parental aspect is what I am referring to in this case. I strongly believe men should lead the home. If a "male" is acting like an idiot or a fool and bringing destruction into the home due to his behavior, he is in no way equipped to lead the family, and by all means we certainly can't define him as a "man." There are many, many successful female leaders born into this world everyday . . . I, myself, am one.

The Seed of Shame

For those reading this book who have had sexual experiences, just stop and think about the first time you did. All first experiences with sexual intercourse are more often than not embarrassing and/or awkward to say the least. It is as simple as that. We can remember the shame over how we did "it" and where we did "it." We blushed when we looked upon our partner's face when it was over. Some have been known to have their hands over their face the duration of the act. For some, the warm fuzzies would get lost in the total humiliation one was feeling over the act itself. Now the shame or embarrassment is usually the first time the cursed or blessed (depending on the circumstances) event takes place.

For women it is especially difficult when she finds herself constantly changing partners. For the most part, after the man has seduced her with a "just be mine tonight" ploy, she is ashamed over the notion that she will be pitched on the discard heap the very next day as her lover moves on to new and uncharted waters. There is so much shame in feeling duped and used. It is still a great mystery ladies, that men seldom have this response as they go from one partner to the next. As a matter of fact, they really rack these up as badges of honor. To add insult to injury don't let the woman become pregnant from her now MIA (Missing In Action) boyfriend, lover, soul mate. She now feels dirty on top of it all. If she doesn't rush to get a quick abortion, which eventually adds more feelings of dirt and guilt, she then walks around for the next seven to eight months with her tummy swelling, unmarried, and wondering what family and friends think of her. Even though we've just come out of the 90's and are now products of this fast-paced 21st century, it's amazing how many young women still try to conceal their pregnancy with loose clothing. She may even stay in the house, stay away from friends, and drop out of school. Some will even buy inexpensive Cubic Zirconia rings to wear on the left hand ring finger so as to pass the ring off as an engagement ring. This makes her "feel better" in the presence of friends and family. Why? Sin always results in shame. Sooner or later the shame always comes.

We clearly see this is what happened with Adam and Eve. She turned to the voice of the enemy and ceased listening to the voice of her Heavenly Father. By so doing, she tied herself and her soul to Adam in such a way it would cause her desire to be for her husband forever (Genesis 3:16b) and no longer for the Living God. What she and Adam once had with God was lost forever. God wanted their total and complete devotion, without limits . . . that was to be no more.

Well . . . I Prefer The Masterpiece

WHAT ABOUT PROCREATION? WE all believe God to be an awesome and powerful God, Amen? Whether our belief came because we heard Him preached, studied the scriptures, or saw some miracle performed, we know He is a Great God! Too often we are all discovering God's way of doing things is so far removed from our finite mind. The Bible says in Isaiah 55:8-9:

> *"For My thoughts are not your thoughts,*
> *Nor are your ways My ways," says the LORD." For as the*
> *heavens are higher than the earth, So are My ways higher than*
> *your ways, And My thoughts than your thoughts."*

We have to keep this in mind when thinking about His ways of multiplicity of mortals here on earth because God does things so differently from how we would do them. Let's see what Genesis 1:26 says about God's established prototype for birth:

> *Then God said, "Let Us make man in Our image, according to*
> *Our likeness; let them have dominion over the fish of the sea, over*
> *the birds of the air, and over the cattle, over all the earth and over*
> *every creeping thing that creeps on the earth."*

I put it to you, should that which has rule and dominion function at a higher realm than that which is ruled and dominated? God is the highest authority in the universe. He certainly functions at a higher realm than the mortals He created. God originally created man to function in a place of dominion that far exceeded that of the plant and animal kingdom. The act of procreation is a carnal, natural act. Yet, we were solely made by God to be spiritual beings. When mortals come together in coitus, they may have heightened emotions and some will venture to say a "spiritual experience", but nevertheless, when we boil it all down it is a natural, carnal act…that takes a great deal of physical work on the part of their flesh and blood body!

Let's take for instance a dog, when a male dog mounts a female dog the sole purpose of the act is to carry out what is intended by nature. The female dog is in her mating season and the male dog is there instinctively to accommodate the female's need, thus the continuance of the species. Why then does some of our coital encounters so closely resemble that of the animal kingdom which we rule and dominate? Why? The reason is when man fell into sin he was also reduced to performing just like those which he was to rule and dominate. He lost his original status and privilege of procreating on a higher plane than the animal kingdom, and fell to a level of carnality like that of the animals. It is as if he was thrown into an express elevator on a fast track from the penthouse suite of spirituality to the sub-basement of carnality. By the way this also happened to someone else we know—Lucifer!

> *I also thought, "As for men, God tests them so that they may see that they are like the animals. Ecclesiastes 3:18 NIV*

Not only does this "GOD-MADE-MANKIND-RULER" have sex on the same level as the animal kingdom, but he is also now terrified of the animals of the kingdom he is to rule. The lions are locked up in zoos and dare they ever escape, the mouse has the entire family terrorized and standing atop the kitchen counter as he scurries around the room, bees and "flying roaches" have people getting into all kinds of car accidents, as they try to fight these beasts while behind the wheel, so who's ruling who? Yes, man is well able to go to the jungles of darkest Africa and capture these wild beasts, put them in steel cages so we may take a peek at them for a price, but for the most part, in this post-fall era, we are afraid of the animals and the animals are afraid of us. In the beginning it was not so, man so well dominated this lesser kingdom, that all the beasts would walk up to him by the mandate of God, and Adam would name each and every one of them with no fear of harm to himself.

We know God creatively spoke man into existence after He creatively spoke everything else into being. He saved the best for last! God never intended for us to be anything less than spiritual beings. We will look at a couple of scriptures, they are John 4:24, and Romans 8:9a:

> *God is Spirit, and those who worship Him must worship in spirit and truth.*

> *But you are not in the flesh but in the Spirit, if indeed the Spirit of God dwells in you.*

I was meditating on this one summer day in 1999, and the Holy Spirit dropped into my spirit this thought, "Who is it to say that just as God put Adam to sleep and pulled out Eve, why couldn't Adam and Eve's spirit speak children into existence and they be pulled out of her as well?" Genesis 1:27 says we are made in His likeness, so why can't we do what He does? These two created beings had dominion, rule, and authority to do what God commanded. They were created from the beginning to do what He did; creatively speak as He did. They had but to speak the Word. Isn't that what we read in John 6:63:

> *It is the Spirit who gives life; the flesh profits nothing. The words that I speak to you are spirit, and they are life.*

Now let's take another good look at this plan of procreation. First of all let's look at the definition of the word. Procreation not only is defined as begetting offspring, to generate, and produce, but it is also defined as "to bring into being." In Genesis 1:3 – 1:26 we see that each and everything God wanted created, He spoke it into existence, He brought it "into being." From the heavens to the earth and everything in between, He spoke and it was so. Now God also made some of the things He had previously spoken into being. The first thing He did was to actively separate the light from the dark. He made two great lights, a greater light for day and a lesser light for the night and set them in the firmament. He created the sea creatures for the waters and winged birds for the air. Lastly, He made the beasts and cattle that were to walk on the earth. When He was done with creating all the plants and animals He spoke a command to them to fill the earth by being fruitful and multiplying after the manner in which He made these lower kingdoms to be fruitful and multiply. From that moment to this they have obediently been doing just that. In Genesis 1:27 we get the sense that God has now moved to create a higher functioning being; a being that is patterned exactly after the image and likeness of Himself. He wanted to create a carbon copy of Himself in the earth. A carbon copy that will procreate as He, God, does. He, therefore, proceeds to take everything about Himself, all of His creative, awesome, miracle producing, spiritual ways, and put it in a package, wrap flesh around it and tell this being to subdue and dominate everything that He, God, has previously made. He also commands this flesh wrapped being to be fruitful and multiply, but He wants Him to do it at the higher level at which He, God, does it. How does God do the fruitful and multiply thing? By doing just what He has shown us. It's right there in Genesis 1:3 – 1:26. He does it by the spirit! When I AM speaks anything into existence…It IS! The Bible says in Romans 4:17:

> (as it is written, "I have made you a father of many nations") in the presence of Him whom he believed--God, who gives life to the dead and calls those things which do not exist as though they did;

The entire universe was in a state of BE NOT (had not come "into being"), before God started speaking. When He was through speaking, everything that formerly WAS NOT…WAS and to this day still IS! If God wanted man to procreate, it was to be in the image and likeness of the way God procreated, not in the image and likeness of the way plants and animals procreate. Adam and Eve were made from the beginning to do what God did! This is why He tells them in Genesis 1:26 how they will procreate…in His image and likeness. In that the fall interrupted everything, we may never really know how awesome a plan God had in place for procreation; but the pain a woman experiences with childbirth, as well as the tendency toward multiplicity of childbirth, was not the original plan of the Father. God was far too awesome and excellent in the way He designed everything than to relegate this plan for childbirth. Remember, Jesus was conceived through a conversation!

Are we talking about the same God who spoke through the mouth of a jackass (Numbers 22:28-30), the same God that brought forth the ten plagues of Egypt (Exodus 7:14-11:5)? Yes! Scientists now through research have found that the ten plagues actually happened in the systematic order in which they occurred. This is the same God that showed up at the doorsteps of a young virgin girl's home in Galilee of Nazareth and had a conversation with her through the mouth of an angel, and she became pregnant! There was no sex to get her pregnant! There was no will of the flesh or some carnal encounter to bring about this spiritual conception. The Spirit of God wanted a spiritually yielded virgin to allow Spirit (God's), and spirit (Mary's), to have intercourse (intercourse means meeting) so that the Son of God could be conceived! How does God get Jesus, the image and likeness of Himself, into Mary's womb? The same way He did everything in Genesis 1:3 – 1:26. I AM speaks and the Son of God IS!

We read about satan deceiving Adam and Eve in the Garden, so in Genesis 3:16a God says:

> *To the woman He said: "I will greatly multiply your sorrow and your conception; In pain you shall bring forth children…."*

I Must Have The Counterfeit

IT WAS NEVER, EVER God's intention that women would experience labor and pain in birthing a baby; some have even suffered death! So we see the end result of their eating from the tree of knowledge was what may have halted the possible plan of God regarding procreation for the human race. This cunning serpent may have been privy to this knowledge, too—he used to dwell in heaven as Lucifer. He knew God had a secret strategy for creating him as well as all the other millions of angels that are still in the presence of God today. Angels that are able to transform themselves into human beings at God's command! We read in Hebrews 13:2 the following:

> *Do not forget to entertain strangers, for by so doing some have unwittingly entertained angels.*

The above scripture makes it apparent that angels have no problem looking just like you and me. This means what is originally in an invisible state of existence to the naked eye can suddenly appear out of nowhere in appearance, just as any other mortal being. Now there is no sex involved in them doing this. They just do it. Not to mention their spiritual authority is lower than ours, because they exist solely to do the will of God and to minister to (serve) the heirs of promise. When these spiritual beings are transformed into human form it is impossible to know the difference. Therefore, what rule or law is there to say that we human beings were meant to exist in the state we find ourselves today? We cannot possibly imagine how it could have been for us, if Adam and Eve had not sinned. Most assuredly we were not meant to be stuck in these bodies that break up when we fall, come "under attack" by our heart when it is mistreated, slowly and painfully corrode when it is overcome with disease and sickness. I have thought so many times about the body Jesus had before He died, and the body He had after He arose. Jesus, Himself, wanted to show off His new resurrected body to His disciples, so what does He do? He just appears out of no where! In John's account in the gospels, John makes a point about the doors being shut to the room where they were:

> *Then the same day at evening, being the first day of the week, when the doors were shut where the disciples were assembled, for fear of the Jews, Jesus came and stood in the midst, and said to them, "Peace be with you." And after eight days His disciples were again inside, and Thomas with them. Jesus came, the doors being shut, and stood in the midst, and said, "Peace to you!"*
> *John 20:19, 26*

When Jesus did these appearances, He wanted the disciples to know this was the type of body they would also look forward to having in the eternal realm. However, there was no way possible that glorified body was to be birthed out of Mary. The only spiritual part Mary could play in the plan of God was to yield her will to His, God's Spirit, and allow a "spiritual conception" to take place. This child, Fathered by God Himself, was to be birthed from a human body just like ours; therefore it was subject to the same birth mandate given to Eve in the book of Genesis. Jesus speaks of two types of births in John 3 and He tells Nicodemus that he must be "born again" if he wants to inherit eternal life. He told Nicodemus that mankind is birthed into the earth the first time when the mother's water breaks, born of the flesh; and is birthed the second time, after receiving Jesus Christ, born of the spirit. Well, likewise, Jesus was birthed the first time by His mother Mary and the second time was after spending 72 hours in the grave:

> *But now Christ has risen from the dead, and has become the first fruits of those who have fallen asleep. For since by man came*

death, by Man also came the resurrection of the dead.

Behold, I tell you a mystery: We shall not all sleep, but we shall be changed...

1 Corinthians 15:20, 21 and 51

We will be changed into what? We will be changed into spiritual beings with the spiritual bodies we were meant to have from the beginning—changed into the body Jesus Christ has, changed into the bodies the angels have, changed into the bodies we should have had in the first place!

Only after Jesus' body was raised up with resurrection power, which is the Spirit of God, was this body going to be the same as Adam and Eve's bodies were before the fall. We were always meant to be spiritual beings and absolutely nothing less. We were also meant to replicate ourselves in the same way, in which Adam and Eve first arrived here, by the Spirit. These are the type of beings God intended would walk in dominion power and authority to subdue the earth, the same physical make-up as angels. We will never become angels; only have the same physical make-up.

When Lucifer, now satan, dwelled in the heavens, he had to have been privy to much revelation and insight regarding God and His power. He could have very well witnessed God's construction process of these two spiritual beings that were to rule Eden. We know all too well how people who are part of the "inner circle" always have all kinds of information that no others know. Remember that Jesus had His three, Peter, James, and John. God had His three, Michael, Gabriel, and Lucifer. Lucifer, however is a permanent Missing In Action angel who will never again regain his status. Once he was aware of this, he decided far be it from him to go it alone. This is when he was victorious in deceiving one-third of the heavenly host who also lost their spiritual positions; but that was not enough, he then went after God's first two precious created human beings as well! As much as was within his power, he was determined to bring all that God had created to utter destruction! In the plan of God, Lucifer was a high ranking arch-angel, a key player in the realm

47

of God's glory. Lucifer understood his purpose and was fulfilling it until, unfortunately, iniquity was found in him. Let's look at Ezekiel 28:15:

> *You were perfect in your ways from the day you were created, till iniquity was found in you.*

Can We Pre-Treat This?

In THE 50'S AND 60'S there was a cute little comic book that many children liked to read, it was titled, *Hot Stuff.* It was about this cute little devil that was bright cherry-red in color with little tiny horns, a pixie tail, and he carried a pitchfork. My older sister, Lucille (now deceased), always seemed to have enough extra spending money to buy the latest comic books, hot off the presses. This was one of her favorites. Naturally when she was finished with the book, I was next in line. I used to enjoy those *Hot Stuff* comic books so much. Guess what? I really thought for the longest that the devil was a red creature with horns, a tail, and a pitch fork . . . like many of you, too!

Even as I became a little older I saw pictures that were gruesome, and certainly not as cute as *Hot Stuff,* but nevertheless I figured satan was grotesque, ugly, and to be feared. I wondered so many times why Eve did not run away when she saw that ugly creature; how could she even talk to him? Today we know that he did not look like the creature from the black lagoon, but quite the contrary. He was an absolutely glorious being filled with more splendor than we could possibly imagine. Let's look at the scriptures that tell us how he looked and what he did as Lucifer:

> *Your pomp is brought down to Sheol,*
> *And the sound of your stringed instruments;*
> *The maggot is spread under you,*
> *And worms cover you.'*
> *"How you are fallen from heaven,*
> *O Lucifer, son of the morning!*
> *How you are cut down to the ground,*

You who weakened the nations!
For you have said in your heart:
'I will ascend into heaven,
I will exalt my throne above the stars of God;
I will also sit on the mount of the congregation
On the farthest sides of the north;
I will ascend above the heights of the clouds,
I will be like the Most High.'
Yet you shall be brought down to Sheol,
To the lowest depths of the Pit."
Isaiah 14:11-15

Therefore thus says the Lord GOD:
"Because you have set your heart as the heart of a god,
Behold, therefore, I will bring strangers against you, the most
terrible of the nations; and they shall draw their swords against
the beauty of your wisdom, and defile your splendor. They shall
throw you down into the Pit, and you shall die the death of the
slain in the midst of the seas.
"Will you still say before him who slays you, 'I am a
god'? But you shall be a man, and not a god, in the hand of him
who slays you. You shall die the death of the uncircumcised by the
hand of aliens; for I have spoken," says the Lord GOD.' "
Moreover the word of the LORD came to me, saying,
"Son of man, take up a lamentation for the king of Tyre, and say
to him, 'Thus says the Lord GOD:
"You were the seal of perfection, Full of wisdom
and perfect in beauty. You were in Eden, the garden of God;
every precious stone was your covering: the sardius, topaz,
and diamond, beryl, onyx, and jasper, sapphire, turquoise, and
emerald with gold. The workmanship of your timbrels and pipes
was prepared for you on the day you were created.
"You were the anointed cherub who covers; I established
you; you were on the holy mountain of God; you walked back and
forth in the midst of fiery stones. You were perfect in your ways
from the day you were created, till iniquity was found in you.
"By the abundance of your trading you became filled
with violence within, and you sinned; therefore I cast you as a
profane thing out of the mountain of God; and I destroyed you,

O covering cherub, from the midst of the fiery stones.
　　"Your heart was lifted up because of your beauty; you corrupted your wisdom for the sake of your splendor; I cast you to the ground, I laid you before kings, that they might gaze at you.
　　"You defiled your sanctuaries by the multitude of your iniquities, by the iniquity of your trading; therefore I brought fire from your midst; it devoured you, and I turned you to ashes upon the earth in the sight of all who saw you. All who knew you among the peoples are astonished at you; you have become a horror, and shall be no more forever." ' "

Ezekiel 28:6-19

In *Strong's Concordance*, iniquity is defined as moral evil; perverseness; unrighteousness; wickedness; to deal unjustly. The word we will focus on at this juncture is perverseness.

Now most people, whether they are Christians or non-Christians, tend to have a real problem with and a pretty low opinion of liars. After all liars just get on the nerves of everyone. We want to know if what they are saying is the truth or not; we want to believe something, sometimes. We all have to admit we have told a lie or two in our lives as well. On the one hand, however, we don't think of liars as the worst of all sinners or "all that bad." We human beings have neatly labeled all sins we commit on this scale of one to twenty. Number one being I'm so close to St. Peter's pearly gates, I can see the streets of gold, and number twenty being, I'm awakened each morning with the pungent smell of sulfur and brimstone wafting through the air of my bedroom, and can almost feel the heat of the fires of hell on my feet! Well, the iniquity found in Lucifer was number twenty plus! His sin was far more wicked than just lying against God. What was found in him was the lowest form of sensuality. What was found in him was perverseness, or as we call it today—perversion! The baser of natures, if you will. This very iniquity found in him is what gave rise to the deception in the Garden of Eden. From the very split second Adam and Eve began to take their fill of this most base of pleasures, this spirit of iniquity began to catapult through the spirit realm at warp speed corrupting all the seed of tomorrow lying inside of Adam. At the same moment, God had to have felt like His very heart was being ripped to shreds within Him when he cried out in anguish to His first created male son, "Where are you?" (Genesis 3:9). In other words, "Your spirit and My Spirit are no longer in the sweet place of communion and love we have always shared, you moved." God must have said to Adam, "When I ran a quick check on Myself, I felt the presence of that same iniquity I ran across with Lucifer when he was here with Me in heaven." It was a very familiar feeling indeed. It was also the same stench of foulness He knew had tainted the atmosphere of His throne room before. God must have cried out, "Oh Adam, how could you!"

We are all very aware of the fact that God originally created Adam and Eve to live forever. If they had not sinned they would have been in the most wonderful state of eternal existence ever, and all mankind after them. We know, however, that was not the case. I then have to ask myself, well why Jesus? Why was Jesus Christ, the Son of God, always in the plan of God? It is because God knew before the foundation of the world that Adam and Eve would blow it! Regardless of the fact that God did not want Adam and Eve to blow it, the truth of the matter is, they did. Well, how did God know that? He is a God that knows all things. He knows the end of a matter from the beginning. God was not going to be taken by surprise with no back–up plan. Likewise, He knew that there needed to be in place a plan for men and women to be sanctified after the fall, after the sexual encounter. God knew that the sexual act would go on until time was no more. He already had a plan in place for the would be perverse act to be made holy and righteous, the marriage covenant. The marriage covenant purifies and makes holy before God what was originally seen as sin. Now the sanctification of sex through marriage is a "must do," but is not actually the paramount issue here. What is always of paramount importance to God is unity; oneness; sameness, as in same purpose. Therefore, what springs out of this marriage covenant is a whole new animal, it's called parents. We read in Genesis 2:24:

Therefore a man shall leave his father and mother and be joined to his wife, and they shall become one flesh.

There were no parents at this point; there were no mothers and fathers. Adam did not have a mother and father, per se, so why does Moses include this narrative at this juncture of the Torah? Moses must have clearly understood there would be a new *modus operandi* instituted by which mankind could come into the presence of God. All any of us would have needed, pre–fall, is our Heavenly Father. Adam may not have fully understood that man and woman would no longer be in a spiritual state of oneness with God as before. In spiritual oneness with God, they would continue to procreate as God did. Once the sin occurred, however, they were going to have to become one with each other in a whole new way, why? "How can two walk together unless they be agreed" (Amos 3:3). When there is unity between man's seed and a woman's seed it produces a baby. The egg agreed to receive the sperm. A baby evidences the unity, the oneness, thereby producing fruits of multiplicity. Fall or no fall, God still had a mandate in place, which was to be fruitful and multiply and God was going to make sure it was fulfilled no matter what it would take. In order to keep His current mandate on the continuum of existence, He in His foreknowledge had this plan in place ahead of time. Isn't God so wonderful? He knows we are going to lose our eternal state, so He already has Jesus Christ in place to win it back. He knows we are going to opt for the lesser plan of procreation, so He already has the marriage covenant in the wings to help us out. What a great God He is!

He Could Moonwalk Better Than Michael

God in all His wisdom had a reason for creating Lucifer as the awesome wonder he was. We have read how glorious his appearance was and as he would go sailing through the heavens he made music as he went (Isaiah 14:11 and Ezekiel 28:13c). He was the anointed covering cherub that had the power to cause God to become so moved by the worship that He, God, would bask in His own glory! Lucifer had authority given to him, by God Himself, to minister to Him. This is the best example of total trust on the part of God, to allow a created being less than Himself to have authority to minister to Him. Doesn't that sound familiar? Almost like the same attitude He has toward us.

We want to take a look at this point of how important music is in the spirit realm. We understand the spirit realm is comprised of two levels. The kingdom of God, which is all that is good and holy, and the kingdom of hell, which is all that is evil and wicked. Music will make a demand on the realm in which it is making a deposit. Therefore, most music in the church is designed to draw us into the presence of the Lord so that we may bask in His love; whereas the music in the night club atmosphere is strictly designed to appease the fleshly desires of man's carnal nature.

It is very apparent in our society today that music has become a multi-billion dollar a year industry. There's music out there to appeal to the taste of each and every person. When people are happy, they play music; when people are sad, they play music. At a time of celebration there is the striking up of the band with loud cymbals and drums. Music is also used to lure thousands and thousands of people each day into lurid sexual encounters. Just as music is a booming business that sells, well so does sex . . . and sells very well I might add. Music and sex are by no means strange bedfellows.

I can remember at the age of 26, I made Jesus Christ Lord of my life. I made a 180-degree turn from the old so I could begin to walk with God, as I should in the new—walk according to the Word of God as a single female. Needless to say, there were some behaviors I had to make drastic decisions about and there was no time to delay. Some of these behaviors took a while to change. I certainly stumbled along the way, but after a while God heard my plea and sent reinforcement. One of the first things I did was to totally revolutionize the social life I had with the opposite sex. This was at the strong suggestion of a very close friend, Ruth. She told me that anytime between 12 midnight and 4:00 a.m. was the bewitching hours. A time when most crimes are committed and evil plans are carried out by the enemy. I knew all one had to do was to awaken each morning and turn on the 7:00 a.m. news to find out this was very true. Many times the evil events of the previous night would make major headlines.

This advice prompted me to make some immediate changes. First, as a single woman living alone, I no longer allowed men to come to my apartment, and most certainly not have them over after dark. Before I changed, it had not been unusual for a guy to come over to my home at about 8:00 p.m. and before we knew it, it was 2:00 a.m. and he would have that settling down for a long winter's nap look in his eye. We would start out looking at a few sitcoms or a mystery movie and once those television shows were over, he would suggest I put some albums on the stereo. That brings me to the second change I had to make. All of my Aretha Franklin, O'Jays, Temptations, Spinners, Al Green, etc., etc., finally had to be put on ice. Ruth said the music would only serve to stir up emotions I would not be able to handle. She even went on to say I no longer needed to listen to that music even when I was home alone. It would only cause me trouble. She was right! As I speak with and minister to women today, all I hear about are these two and three a.m. visits by men to the homes of women. These visits have a name, for which the more shielded set (sheltered, inexperienced) reading this book may not be aware. These visits are usually for the express purpose of couples engaging in sexual activity, which is usually accompanied by music as a mood-altering backdrop. These visits are termed "booty calls."

Part Three

Knowledge is of two kinds.
We know a subject ourselves, or we know
where we can find information about it.
—Samuel Johnson

The Best Way To Get There Is To Go

WELL, WHAT DOES THE Lord have to say in His Word regarding sexual behavior of those that are single and those that are married? We read in 1 Corinthians 6:12 – 20:

> *All things are lawful for me, but all things are not helpful. All things are lawful for me, but I will not be brought under the power of any. Foods for the stomach and the stomach for foods, but God will destroy both it and them. Now the body is not for sexual immorality but for the Lord, and the Lord for the body. And God both raised up the Lord and will also raise us up by His power. Do you not know that your bodies are members of Christ? Shall I then take the members of Christ and make them members of a harlot? Certainly not! Or do you not know that he who is joined to a harlot is one body with her? For "the two," He says, "shall become one flesh." But he who is joined to the Lord is one spirit with Him. Flee sexual immorality. Every sin that a man does is outside the body, but he who commits sexual immorality sins against his own body. Or do you not know that your body is the temple of the Holy Spirit who is in you, whom you have from God, and you are not your own? For you were bought at a price; therefore glorify God in your body and in your spirit, which are God's.*

A Christian single has no choice but to run, literally flee from any sexual impropriety. The Word clearly points out a problem with this behavior being manifested in a body that also warehouses the Holy Ghost. These behaviors are most certainly diametrically opposed to one another. It's mixing light with darkness and good with evil. It's the holy and profane, the oil and water! They do not mix! Again, as I look back at my beginning stages of walking out this single lifestyle, God was faithful to give me some much needed help along the lines of deliverance. My good intentions to walk out this Christian lifestyle were certainly met with challenges, but God wanted me to succeed in my endeavors. God therefore orchestrated my meeting a man of God, Pastor James E. Blue of Cincinnati, Ohio, who was introduced to me by my friend Ruth (at that time she was a deaconess in the church he pastors). She and he met with me at my apartment and boy oh boy did I get my first introduction to a true spiritual cleaning out! By the time they left my home that evening, I hardly even knew what had hit me! He started off by taking authority over demonic forces in my life and in my soul; next he began speaking to the atmosphere of my apartment and commanded it to get in order; last, but not least, he began to verbally dismantle all the unhealthy relationships and soul-ties I had. I'm telling you, I was immediately starting to feel brand new and the brand new was frightening! I did not know this Barbara they left me with. I had to get to know her!

I want to also add that as a favor to me at Ruth's suggestion they came to my home, but we all know that this kind of ministry is going to ordinarily take place in the church. I also was instructed by Ruth before Pastor Blue came to my home, to read cover to cover the book, *Pigs In The Parlor*, and also fast and pray. This was in preparation for what God knew I needed to have done. Even though I was then still a member at the Baptist church, I needed spiritual tools to get a spiritual deliverance from wicked spiritual powers. Nothing short of a spiritually capable team, hand picked by God and sent to me to do a spiritual work, not a religious work, would enable me to begin the process of walking like a Christian should walk. Shucks! That is almost like God sending Ananais to Saul at the house on the street called Straight! Praise God!

This Stuff Is High Voltage

Now the Lord says in 1 Corinthians 7:34 that the unmarried

virgin, male or female, cares for the things of the Lord; that he or she may be holy in both body and spirit. Why would the Word speak of food and sex in 1 Corinthians 6:13 and then switch to God's resurrection power that raised Jesus Christ from the dead in 1 Corinthians 6:14? Paul proceeds from there to discuss immoral sexual behavior in 1 Corinthians 6:15-18. Let's take a look at those scriptures and try to get an understanding of Paul's progression of thought:

> *Foods for the stomach and the stomach for foods, but God will destroy both it and them. Now the body is not for sexual immorality but for the Lord, and the Lord for the body. And God both raised up the Lord and will also raise us up by His power. Do you not know that your bodies are members of Christ? Shall I then take the members of Christ and make them members of a harlot? Certainly not! Or do you not know that he who is joined to a harlot is one body with her? For "the two," He says, "shall become one flesh." But he who is joined to the Lord is one spirit with Him. Flee sexual immorality. Every sin that a man does is outside the body, but he who commits sexual immorality sins against his own body.*

This scripture is of utmost importance to understand if we are to get a revelation of a key component of the power in which we, the church, are to walk in these last days of the church. It is necessary to understand that the stomach, which hungers for food, is in the area of our loins. The sexual cravings that our bodies have are in the area of our loins. Does it at all surprise you that when we pray for people and minister to people by and through the anointing, it too springs from the area of our loins? We read in John 7:38, "He that believeth on me, as the scripture hath said, out of his belly shall flow rivers of living water (King James Version)."

Now you can readily see that I referenced the King James Version (KJV) with regard to John 7:38 as opposed to my usual usage of the New King James Version (NKJV). In the KJV the word 'belly' is used versus the word 'heart' in the NKJV. The reason for this interchange of word usage is because the spiritual heart of a man is his belly! It is so common for us as Christians, to put our hands over our physical heart when we speak about our desires for God or our longings as it pertains to spiritual matters, just as we do when saying the Pledge of Allegiance to the flag. However, the heart of a Christian is in the belly, in the loins, in the area where all life is reproduced. No wonder it is imperative that the entire area between the stomach and the thighs must be kept under control. We have to begin to truly see the importance of bringing the body into obedience, and make it subject to obey the spirit man within. We can no longer tolerate the yielding to every desire that our soul craves. Our cravings come out of our loins, out of our belly, but the Bible tells us to " . . . gird our loins with truth," (Ephesians 6:14b). Have you, too, wondered why the first area Paul tells us to spiritually protect in Ephesians 6 is the region of the loins? Why did he not just start with the helmet and work his way down to the shodding of the feet? He could not go against what is a standard practice in scripture. Scripture has always had a pattern of denoting things/people from the most important to the least. Paul denoted, first, the area where we have our greatest battle with our flesh! It's usually the weakest area of all. This is the area where we are the most out of control. The same area where Adam and Eve blew it!

Therefore, as the Word of God begins to rule our lives and we enter into a true intimate relationship with our Heavenly Father, it will become the offshoot of what will be birthed from us. We will be so impregnated with the presence of God that it will form a miracle producing power within us that will open blind eyes, heal the sick and raise the dead. It is the same power that raised Jesus Christ from the dead! This area of our temple is so sacred and important to God that we absolutely must get our temples holy and keep them holy! It is God's earnest desire for His people. This must be done.

My earnest desire for writing this book was to bring out two major points:

1.) *Sex was the sin that caused the initial fall of man*

from God's grace and glory.

2.) *Sex is the fleshly act that the Church must get total authority over so as to assist the ushering in of the return of the Lord. Also before the return of the Lord, the Church must loose an anointing of power and demonstration this world has not seen in the church since the book of Acts! It will no longer just be anointing; it will be HIS GLORY!*

But What About My Needs

PAUL MAKES A POINT regarding his own preference in 1 Corinthians 7:7; he desires that singles would be as he was. Paul had the gift of celibacy in operation in his life, and that was a choice he made for Christ. Some Bible Scholars believe that there had to have been a time when Paul was married. It is believed that he was a member of the Sanhedrin Council, and because of Jewish law and custom, only married men were allowed to be seated on the Sanhedrin Council. Whether or not he had become a widower, just left the marriage, "or his wife left him when he became a Christian" is not documented, but what we do know is he made a decision to become celibate as an act of service to the Lord. In 1 Corinthians 7 Paul gives directives for the married as well as the single as it pertains to sex. What is of key importance, however, is this little opening comment he makes in 1 Corinthians that much of the church has glossed over as perhaps being insignificant to the church at large. The comment is so powerful on it's own, however, that Paul uses it as a segue into all he addresses on the subject of singleness and marriage. We read in 1 Corinthians 7:1:

> "Now concerning the things of which you wrote to me: It is good
> for a man not to touch a woman."

Do we really understand how powerful that statement is in light of all that God has revealed to us? John the Baptist didn't touch a woman sexually; Jesus Christ didn't touch a woman sexually; Paul ceased to be involved sexually with a woman. He even gives directives for those who cannot maintain self-control with regards to sex in 1

Corinthians 7:9. There he encourages marriage as the option.

> *"But if they cannot exercise self-control, let them marry. For it is better to marry than to burn with passion."*

Jesus never knew a woman; so the subject of 1 Corinthians 7:9 was not an issue of concern. We know according to scripture, Jesus had many female followers. He effectively ministered to women on a regular basis and never committed any sin, but even more, no sexual sin at all. By the same token, women adored Him and they in turn ministered to many of His needs as well. Jesus was very much married to fulfilling His Father's purpose for His life and was bound to that vision with every fiber of His being. That is why He could walk out 1 Corinthians 6:17 with God, His Father!

> *But he who is joined to the Lord is one spirit with Him.*

Paul addresses one aspect of the Body of Christ in 1 Corinthians 6:13 after making singles aware that the necessity for food and a proper attitude toward sex is of the utmost importance. He further states in 1 Corinthians 7:5 that married couples while fasting will abstain from food and sex for an agreed upon period of time.

It is my hope the following scriptures will reveal a direct link between sexual purity, abstinence of sex in marriage (when fasting), and when single the abstinence of sex as a lifestyle. This has a direct affect on the power of the anointing that must come back to the church at large! As we all become more conscientious about our bodies as temples of the Holy Ghost, we will be in absolute awe of the type of anointing we will begin to warehouse within us for His kingdom!

Once Upon A Time

*L*ET'S LOOK AT OLD Testament scriptures as well as New Testament scriptures to further unlock this mystery.

Moses In The Mountain With God

> *Now when the people saw that Moses delayed coming down from the mountain, the people gathered together to Aaron, and said to him, "Come, make us gods that shall go before us; for as for this Moses, the man who brought us up out of the land of Egypt, we do not know what has become of him." And Aaron said to them, "Break off the golden earrings which are in the ears of your wives, your sons, and your daughters, and bring them to me." So all the people broke off the golden earrings which were in their ears, and brought them to Aaron. And he received the gold from their hand, and he fashioned it with an engraving tool, and made a molded calf. Then they said, "This is your god, O Israel, that brought you out of the land of Egypt!" So when Aaron saw it, he built an altar before it. And Aaron made a proclamation and said, "Tomorrow is a feast to the LORD." Then they rose early on the next day, offered burnt offerings, and brought peace offerings; and the people sat down to eat and drink, and rose up to play. - Exodus 32:1-6*

In the account of Moses, we know that Moses spent forty days and forty nights in the mountain of the Lord. He fasted before Him (Exodus 24:18) as he prepared to receive the commandments of God. In the meantime, the enemy had the children of Israel in a "party over here" mode because Moses delayed coming down from the mountain. What were they doing at their party? They were engaging in eating, drinking and sex! Now the sex they engaged in ran the full gamut of sexual pleasures. They were fulfilling every base desire their hearts imagined. We have to keep in mind that there is sex, then THERE IS SEX! While we are grateful that after the fall God made provision to sanctify sex and make it holy by instituting the covenant of marriage as the purifying agent, let us be mindful that all acts committed under the heading of SEX are not sanctioned by God.

In the New Testament scriptures there are several references to a word that speaks of UNRESTRAINED sex. The word is lasciviousness. Galatians 5:19 says, "Now the works of the flesh are manifest, which are these; Adultery, fornication, uncleanness, lasciviousness . . .." KJV

> *Unger's Bible Dictionary cites the Greek 'aselgeia, that which "excites disgust". A KJV term referring to unbridled lust, licentiousness, and wantonness. See Sensuality.*

Now we already know that adultery and fornication are sexual sins within themselves. Why does the Bible make mention of uncleanness and lasciviousness if there were not other means by which people could sin regarding sexual behaviors? The Bible says the marriage bed is holy:

> *Marriage is honorable among all, and the bed undefiled; Hebrews 13:4*

However holy the marriage bed is, it is not going to remain holy by those persons who drag into it whips, chains, dogs, and any of those kinds of aides their deviant little hearts so desire!

The Bible says in Exodus 32:25 the people were totally unrestrained . . . no limits! Also, it is interesting to note that Joshua said there was the "sound of war in the camp." He could tell the sound was not of victory or defeat, but the sound of pleasure (Exodus 32:

18-19). They were also singing and dancing. Could this have been the type of dancing Salome did in Mark 6? What they were doing made God very angry, and to top it all off, they commissioned the making of the golden calf! More than likely there was sexual impropriety with the idol as well. Idolatry is always linked with sexual immorality. We will read scriptures about that later.

When Moses came down from the mountain after fasting and praying, he was equipped with the Word of God engraved on stone . . . ALL the law of God had been given to him. He sacrificed himself in fasting and prayer and BANG, God released information to him that had never been given before. Brand new instruction and direction from the Lord. This information came to him because he made a decision to eat no food and have no sex for a season. Many times we must be in a state of sanctity if we want deeper things from the Lord. Another good nugget of truth to look at in regard to God's command for sanctity is in Exodus 19:15; 20:22-26:

> *And he said to the people, "Be ready for the third day; do not come near your wives."*

> *Then the LORD said to Moses, "Thus you shall say to the children of Israel: 'You have seen that I have talked with you from heaven. You shall not make anything to be with Me—gods of silver or gods of gold you shall not make for yourselves. An altar of earth you shall make for Me, and you shall sacrifice on it your burnt offerings and your peace offerings, your sheep and your oxen. In every place where I record My name I will come to you, and I will bless you. And if you make Me an altar of stone, you shall not build it of hewn stone; for if you use your tool on it, you have profaned it. Nor shall you go up by steps to My altar, that your nakedness may not be exposed on it."*

God wanted it to be very clear, not only were His people not to have other gods besides Himself (idolatry), but He wanted to make sure His people would not be climbing all over His altar with their sexual selves! He wanted no sexual immorality! We have to be very plain spoken here. In the Old Testament God lists laws that address body secretions and how persons are unclean for an appointed period of time when they have them, or if they have been in contact with secretions from other persons. When men had vaginal secretions on their penis, or women had semen ejaculated into their vaginas, according to the law, they were unclean. In other words, the altar would no longer be clean and pure; therefore, rendering God unable to approach it or draw near. In that the people were given to perverse sexual appetites, on top of it all, God was basically saying, "My altar will end up profaned during your times of worship before I could ever draw near!" God has been waiting so long to finally find the worshippers He has always wanted. As Jesus said in John 4:23-24:

> *But the hour is coming, and now is, when the true worshipers will worship the Father in spirit and truth; for the Father is seeking such to worship Him. God is Spirit, and those who worship Him must worship in spirit and truth.*

Let us look at some other stories in the Bible. These illustrations will show how the main characters in the story and their personal decision of a "no sex for a season" policy positively affected Bible history. We will start with the story of David and Uriah.

When David And Uriah Dined
2 Samuel 11:1-27

This was a time to go to war, but the devil was up to his same old tricks, so he seduced David into staying home from the battle. In the process of time David ended up on the palace rooftop and he just so happened to see Bathsheba bathing. Well, well, well what a coincidence. So here we have the King of Israel, who is highly anointed to rule and reign as well as defeat his every enemy in battle (who by the way received arduous praise of the same), duped into the temptation of adultery with the wife of one of his own loyal soldiers who is away at the battle—a battle in which he himself, should have been fighting.

As always, man plus woman equals baby. So, the plot thickens. David receives the news of Bathsheba's pregnancy. David must now figure out a cover-up. He plans to have Uriah, Bathsheba's husband, come in from battle and go and lie with his wife. Who could have believed the integrity of this mighty man of valor, Uriah! Uriah has been called out of the battle and has a golden opportunity for what surely was some much needed rest and relaxation, but instead he says to his King, "The ark of Israel and Judah are dwelling in tents, and my lord Joab and the servants of my lord are encamped in the open fields. Shall I then go to my house to eat and drink, to lie with my wife? As you live and as your soul lives, I will not do this thing." (2 Samuel 11:11). Can you believe it? Uriah slept on King David's doorstep that night instead of going home to his wife! He clearly understood not to eat, drink, or have sex!

The devil never gets tired of, "if at first you don't succeed, try, try again." So he has David wait a couple of days and then David personally oversees Uriah's eating and drinking, so as to get him drunk. Then David attempts to send Uriah to bed down with Bathsheba again. What does Uriah do? He goes to sleep it off in the servants' quarters, and refuses to go home! (2 Sam. 11:13). Here we have a man not void at all of understanding the need to guard the anointing that is camped out in a tent. He's so concerned about protecting the anointing (ark) he lays aside all notions of fulfilling fleshly desires. Oh! Uriah is good . . . I mean he is real good! Where are the men like him today? The ark and men's lives are at stake, so he chooses, by an act of his own will, to fast from sex!

Ahasuerus' Queens
Esther 1:1-4:16

In reading this book of the Bible, many of us are very familiar with the famous cry of Queen Esther as she prepared for her fast, " . . . I will go to the King, which is against the law; and if I perish, I perish! (Esther 4:16b)."

What we may not know, however, was the need for God to right a grave spiritual injustice that was to be predicated upon the women of Shushan and the surrounding provinces. She would not only save the women of the province in which she lived, but the Jewish nation as well.

We start by reading about this seven day feast being given by King Ahasuerus. You talk about "get down tonight." This was an extremely important soiree! This comes after a 180 day political "dog and pony show" for all the powers to be in the surrounding kingdoms. This would be comparable to our presidential campaign for the White House right on through to the Inaugural Ball at the end of the presidential race, with everything that goes on in between. Well, Queen Vashti decided she wanted to celebrate with some of her women friends so, she too, had a feast. So what do you think happened? As always, when one begins to "tie one on," they begin to let it all hang out. Hence, some of the strangest and lewdest behaviors we humans are capable of, like cream, rises to the top. According to scripture, the seventh and last day of this big luau the King's heart becomes merry with wine. He decides to request the ultimate absurdity. He requested, "eh' excuse me," he commanded the seven eunuchs to bring his wife to him wearing the royal crown, so as to show her beauty off to his many lusty awaiting male guests. Now be it far from me to say that Vashti was in total rebellion against the King when she refused to come. She had every right to refuse to come, if the invitation was based on her showing off "all of her beauty." I believe what the King wanted to do was to show off her royal crown atop a partially or totally nude body! The scripture alludes to the fact that he commands the Queen to come. Why could he not just invite her to come and enjoy sharing her presence with his friends? Why does it necessitate his sending seven men to go and get her? Many times people will get into very irrational behaviors and make pretty ugly demands after becoming intoxicated. Wouldn't that be too much for any wife to take from her husband? Why do you think she refused? First of all, sending seven eunuchs was a guarantee these men would not be touching the Queen. They could also form a human shield, of sorts, about her nudity as they escorted her into the presence of the King. Lastly, it doesn't take seven men to go and get one woman! No wife would refuse to allow her husband's friends to see her beauty shown off in a decent and presentable fashion. That would be the epitome of flattery, to say the least. This other request, however, was a far too extreme demand her husband was making of her. Well, in short order, Vashti was banished from the presence of the King for the remainder of her days. The King soon desired to take another wife. Enters the soon to be Queen Esther, stage right.

Now remember what I said previously in the book,

◦✥◦

F OR EVERY ACT OF SIN OR UNRIGHTEOUSNESS DONE, IT MUST BE COUNTERED WITH AN ACT OF RIGHTEOUSNESS EQUAL TO OR GREATER THAN AND CONTRARY TO THE ACT OF SIN DONE, IN ORDER TO CANCEL ITS AUTHORITY.

◦✥◦

Haman has hatched a wicked plot to have all Jews killed. Word of this plot eventually gets to Queen Esther. It is her cousin Mordecai that speaks to her and reminds her of her roots as a Jew. He strongly suggests that it is probably the providential hand of God that had her born for such a time as this to save her people. He tells her she must tell the King of this wicked plot, because she can in no wise keep this thing hidden. This was especially difficult for Queen Esther to do. The King had not seen anyone in thirty days, and to appear before him unsummoned could mean certain death! Nevertheless, just like our God, He gives Queen Esther a revelation as to what to do. She sends word to her cousin, Mordecai, and says, "Go, gather all the Jews, who are present in Shushan, and fast for me; neither eat nor drink for three days, night or day. My maids and I will fast likewise." (Esther 4:16a) Now let's keep in mind and it goes without saying that for Queen Esther, sexual abstinence is factored in as well, after all she had not seen the King for thirty days plus.

What's the end result? The plot is uncovered and Haman is killed and the nation of Jews are saved. God knew of the power of the anointing that would be warehoused within Queen Esther. He knew it would have the authority to cause King Ahasuerus to extend the golden scepter.

Do we really understand what power and anointing would be in the church if we were moving into this same kind of corporate unity of fasting and prayer? Do we realize how our King of kings would extend His scepter in our nation or in the world if the church could get a revelation of flowing in this level of sacrifice by fasting and praying? It would be awesome! Don't forget, Esther, unlike us, did not have the indwelling of the Holy Spirit as we do today!

Idolatry Slips In

But King Solomon loved many foreign women, as well as the daughter of Pharaoh: women of the Moabites, Ammonites, Edomites, Sidonians, and Hittites—from the nations of whom the LORD had said to the children of Israel, "You shall not intermarry with them, nor they with you. Surely they will turn away your hearts after their gods." Solomon clung to these in love. And he had seven hundred wives, princesses, and three hundred concubines; and his wives turned away his heart. For it was so, when Solomon was old, that his wives turned his heart after other gods; and his heart was not loyal to the LORD his God, as was the heart of his father David. For Solomon went after Ashtoreth the goddess of the Sidonians, and after Milcom the abomination of the Ammonites. Solomon did evil in the sight of the LORD, and did not fully follow the LORD, as did his father David. Then Solomon built a high place for Chemosh the abomination of Moab, on the hill that is east of Jerusalem, and for Molech the abomination of the people of Ammon. And he did likewise for all his foreign wives, who burned incense and sacrificed to their gods. So the LORD became angry with Solomon, because his heart had turned from the LORD God of

Israel, who had appeared to him twice, and had commanded him concerning this thing, that he should not go after other gods; but he did not keep what the LORD had commanded. Therefore the LORD said to Solomon, "Because you have done this, and have not kept My covenant and My statutes, which I have commanded you, I will surely tear the kingdom away from you and give it to your servant. Nevertheless I will not do it in your days, for the sake of your father David; I will tear it out of the hand of your son. However I will not tear away the whole kingdom; I will give one tribe to your son for the sake of my servant David, and for the sake of Jerusalem which I have chosen."

1 *Kings 11:1 – 13*

Well, here you have it. Solomon not only disobeyed the command of God to not intermarry with foreign women, but he had lots and lots of foreign women. Solomon was said to have clung to these women in love. Unfortunately, the clinging to the women also meant clinging to their gods. The end result was that Solomon no longer had a loyal heart toward God (verse 4). Why is this important? There is usually an association between idolatry and sexuality, as we read in the account of Moses and the children of Israel. We will see this is the biggest issue plaguing the church today, which we will read in later chapters.

Before moving on to New Testament scriptures, I want to make a small disclaimer here. I am by no means suggesting the entire church body, single or married, give up the need for the pleasure found in sexual fulfillment. Christian single people are not to **know** the pleasure of sex, only married people. When that can of worms was opened in the Garden, God did His part by driving Adam and Eve out of the Garden so that they would not eat of the tree of life. This would have caused them to live forever. They would have opened the door for mankind to make whoopee forever; hence it would have forfeited the ultimate plan of God that Jesus Christ spoke of in Matthew 22:30, "For in the resurrection they neither marry nor are given in marriage, but are like angels of God in heaven." God also needed to sanctify the act so as to allow his children to engage in sexual activity without being in a continual act of sin. God, therefore, lists the rules and regulations in the law that man would have to obey if he were going to engage in sexual activity. All these rules apply to sexual relations within the bounds of marriage only. The marriage covenant is the only covenant that purifies sex. So listen up guys, do all that you want to do now "because when it's over, it's over!" We will do in the eternal realm just about every activity known to man this side of glory with the exception of crying and sexual fulfillment. This in itself is a great revelation, since we spend so much time crying over being sexually unfulfilled (smile)!

Today, like never before, we Christians need to get the whole sexual issue together. We have gone from one extreme end of the spectrum to the other. On the one end we are uptight about discussing it in mixed company under the rafters of The House of God. We have gone to total overload on the other end of the spectrum by spending an obsessive amount of time being sexually stimulated in those internet "chatrooms," or slipping off to those one horse towns off of the highway, 30-50 miles from home, where we can sneak into adult porno shops and purchase or rent every book, video, or toy our soul craves. This has been the result of the church blushing so much over the whole issue instead of allowing healthy dialogue to be established. From the pulpit to the pews we should be addressing these hidden issues which people deal with on a far too regular basis.

A Meeting At The Sacred Table
Anna the Prophetess

And when eight days were completed for the circumcision of the Child, His name was called JESUS, the name given by the angel before He was conceived in the womb.

Now when the days of her purification according to the law of Moses were completed, they brought Him to Jerusalem to present Him to the Lord (as it is written in the law of the Lord, "Every male who opens the womb shall be called holy to the

LORD"), and to offer a sacrifice according to what is said in the law of the Lord, "A pair of turtledoves or two young pigeons."

And behold, there was a man in Jerusalem whose name was Simeon, and this man was just and devout, waiting for the Consolation of Israel, and the Holy Spirit was upon him. And it had been revealed to him by the Holy Spirit that he would not see death before he had seen the Lord's Christ. So he came by the Spirit into the temple. And when the parents brought in the Child Jesus, to do for Him according to the custom of the law, he took Him up in his arms and blessed God and said: "Lord, now You are letting Your servant depart in peace, according to Your word; For my eyes have seen Your salvation which You have prepared before the face of all peoples, a light to bring revelation to the Gentiles, and the glory of Your people Israel."

And Joseph and His mother marveled at those things which were spoken of Him. Then Simeon blessed them, and said to Mary His mother, "Behold, this Child is destined for the fall and rising of many in Israel, and for a sign which will be spoken against (yes, a sword will pierce through your own soul also), that the thoughts of many hearts may be revealed."

Now there was one, Anna, a prophetess, the daughter of Phanuel, of the tribe of Asher. She was of a great age, and had lived with a husband seven years from her virginity; and this woman was a widow of about eighty-four years, who did not depart from the temple, but served God with fastings and prayers night and day. And coming in that instant she gave thanks to the Lord, and spoke of Him to all those who looked for redemption in Jerusalem. Luke 2:21-38

I was so amazed when these scriptures leaped out at me! I've read this passage so many, many times; yet not until I started writing this book, did this make sense to me. Why in the world would the Lord want to make a point of telling us that she had been with her then deceased husband, from her virginity? What did the taking note of Anna being a widow after only seven years of marriage have to do with God introducing her to us as a prophetess from the tribe of Asher? At the time when she was still a young woman, by an act of her own will she made a decision not to remarry therefore giving up the need for sexual relations, but opted for a celibate lifestyle at a time when she, by Jewish standards, was not considered a "widow indeed." What was of paramount importance to her was to serve the Lord. So for over sixty years she never departed from the temple, but served God with fastings and prayers night and day . . . and then Bingo! She is lead by the Spirit, in an "instant," to the place where Simeon, Mary, and Joseph are in the temple. Perhaps she overheard the prophetic word Simeon spoke to Mary, and her heart must have leaped with joy! To know she was one of the very ones that so had the presence of the Lord in her life, that God picked her, along with Simeon, to be the privileged two to behold with their eyes the salvation of Israel! Hallelujah! What an amazing moment in time this had to be! Mary and Joseph had not been sexually involved as of yet. They stand in the temple ceremonially pure and clean, with The Son of God, The Salvation of Israel, The Light to the Gentiles cradled in their arms and in comes these pure ones—Simeon and Anna, who have waited on and served God with their very lives. What a holy, beautiful, and consecrated moment this had to have been at the table of circumcision. To top it off, she is the mouth piece and prophetic evangelist, so to speak, God uses to tell all who were looking for the redemption in Jerusalem, "Listen up Israel, He's here!"

Oh, what fasting and prayer won't get for us as we consecrate ourselves to God. It is no wonder Paul pleaded in Romans 12:1-2:

I beseech you therefore, brethren, by the mercies of God, that you present your bodies a living sacrifice, holy, acceptable to God, which is your reasonable service. And do not be conformed to this world, but be transformed by the renewing of your mind, that you may prove what is that good and acceptable and perfect will of God.

Showdown In The Garden!
Mary Magdalene

IN THE NEW TESTAMENT scriptures, the first strong position taken by the church with regard to sexual impropriety is in the book of Acts. Before we look at the early church, let's take a look at the final deathblow to satan and his kingdom by Jesus Christ, which brings the ultimate victory over what happened in the Garden of Eden.

This revelation was so vivid to me as God unfolded it. I tried to imagine it, as it must have happened. Remember when God spoke to Adam and Eve in the Garden of Eden and explained to them their lot in life, which was also to be for all mankind. To ensure there would be no foul-ups, though, God had to place cherubim at the East of the Garden of Eden with a flaming sword that guarded the tree of life (Genesis 3:24). So man's first hope of eternal bliss with God ends with Adam and Eve being driven out of the Garden of Eden forever and into a life that would now experience drudgery and pain. In this writer's opinion, and not unlike God, the Garden of Eden was left as some unfinished business on the agenda of God. He definitely intended to get back to it sooner or later. The later had finally arrived. It is called "in-the-fullness-of-time." Our scene opens in a garden. Let's read John 19:38-42, with the emphasis on verse 41:

> After this, Joseph of Arimathea, being a disciple of Jesus, but secretly, for fear of the Jews, asked Pilate that he might take away the body of Jesus; and Pilate gave him permission. So he came and took the body of Jesus. And Nicodemus, who at first came to Jesus by night, also came, bringing a mixture of myrrh and aloes, about a hundred pounds. Then they took the body of Jesus, and bound it in strips of linen with the spices, as the

custom of the Jews is to bury. Now in the place where He was crucified there was a garden, and in the garden a new tomb in which no one had yet been laid. So there they laid Jesus, because of the Jews' Preparation Day, for the tomb was nearby.

Look at God! Man's ultimate fall was in the Garden. God's masterful plan set the stage for the culminating events to be set where? In an area that had a garden! Jesus Christ is not only suffering a physical death, the *crucifixion, but a spiritual death for every one of us human beings born into sin, as well.* Unlike Adam and Eve, He's not going to be driven out of this location that contains a garden; but the mandate by God is for Him, who was victorious over sin, to be buried in the garden in a borrowed tomb. The first Adam was driven out of the Garden; the second Adam, however, takes spiritual dominion over the garden and over the tomb and is buried right where He and satan finish the first round of the match.

Now again, John points out that located near the place where Jesus is crucified and dies is a garden and a tomb. I believe the location of the crucifixion is not only God-ordained, but strategically God-ordained. As Jesus is hanging on the tree, perhaps He is able to glimpse in an area not far from Him, a garden...this represents to Him the place of Adam and Eve's death and the death of all mankind, purchased through their disobedience. He is canceling the debt on and becoming a ransom for an eternal death, while He yet hangs there in agonizing pain. Perhaps through His dazed and listless eyes He turns in the other direction and sees a tomb, a tomb He surely must know, being all-knowing, is for Himself. Yet, He is very aware of the fact that all of mankind forever and ever would be sentenced to these cold, dead graves eternally if He was not able to champion our cause right then and there. In His heart He knew there was no turning back from here, this event could not be postponed and He knew this could not be canceled.

O Death, where is your sting?
O Hades, where is your victory?
1 Corinthians 15:55

I tell you where the sting of death and the victory of the grave was, it was being consumed and strangled in the body of our Savior as He hung there; "Death is swallowed up in victory." (1 Corinthians 15:54).

Jesus is certainly aware of the magnitude of what is being spiritually accomplished, as He hangs on the tree, and with that thought alone in mind, He then absolutely refuses to come down! He knows three days and three nights from this point, He and satan will be going for round two!

It is the dawning of the Resurrection Sunday, NOT Easter! Resurrection Sunday has been traditionally referred to as Easter. However, historically, Easter is the goddess of fertility. Fertility is the reason we have associated candy bunnies and baby chicks with Easter. Easter was a pagan goddess of worship which has absolutely nothing to do with Jesus Christ being raised from the dead! It's just like satan to have us blinded to believe that the most holy and sacred of all holidays for the Christians is being associated with a goddess whose onus is to perpetuate sexual sin! Yuck, yuck, double yuck! Let's read John 20:1-10:

> On the first day of the week Mary Magdalene went to the tomb early, while it was still dark, and saw that the stone had been taken away from the tomb. Then she ran and came to Simon Peter, and to the other disciple, whom Jesus loved, and said to them, "They have taken away the Lord out of the tomb, and we do not know where they have laid Him." Peter therefore went out, and the other disciple, and were going to the tomb. So they both ran together, and the other disciple outran Peter and came to the tomb first. And he, stooping down and looking in, saw the linen cloths lying there; yet he did not go in. Then Simon Peter came, following him, and went into the tomb; and he saw the linen cloths lying there, and the handkerchief that had been around His head, not lying with the linen cloths, but folded together in a place by itself. Then the other disciple, who came to the tomb first, went in also; and he saw and believed. For as yet they did not know the Scripture, that He must rise again from the dead. Then the disciples went away again to their own homes.

Mary has run to the tomb early, while it was still dark, expecting to find the body of her beloved Jesus. As she approached the tomb, she found the stone had been rolled away and she is most likely in sheer panic. She immediately runs to seek help from the disciples. They come to see for themselves, and find it as Mary says, an empty tomb. They go inside to examine, yet the full revelation of the scriptures, that He would rise again, is still not apparent to them at this point, so what do the good ole' boys do? Leave and go back home.

As we read John 20:1-10 it gives us some important background information regarding what is about to take place. I'll detour here for a minute and say let us not forget about satan. We understand according to scripture, he is probably figuring out he's blown it big time. The Bible says in 1 Corinthians 2:7-8:

> *But we speak the wisdom of God in a mystery, the hidden wisdom which God ordained before the ages for our glory, which none of the rulers of this age knew; for had they known, they would not have crucified the Lord of glory.*

Now that satan is getting the revelation of his losing battle he is about to stage one last attempt at making a mockery of what God has been so carefully orchestrating for several thousand years. On the enemy's part, your veritable Custer's last stand, but oh no, devil . . . not so fast! Remember that Adam and Eve had pure fellowship with and worship of God in the Garden of Eden, but satan slipped in and caused the spirit of deception to trick Eve. As we read the next few verses we see the stage is being set for one of the greatest power moves on God's part ever!

Here in this garden setting we have Mary, the disciples have gone home and we also have present a man who Mary believes to be the gardener. At this time also, there surely must be an awesome omnipresence of Almighty God as He is overseeing these final moments before His Son ascends from earth to heaven. Let's read John 20:11-18:

But Mary stood outside by the tomb weeping, and as she wept she stooped down and looked into the tomb. And she saw two angels in white sitting, one at the head and the other at the feet, where the body of Jesus had lain. Then they said to her, "Woman, why are you weeping?" She said to them, "Because they have taken away my Lord, and I do not know where they have laid Him." Now when she had said this, she turned around and saw Jesus standing there, and did not know that it was Jesus. Jesus said to her, "Woman, why are you weeping? Whom are you seeking?" She, supposing Him to be the gardener, said to Him, "Sir, if You have carried Him away, tell me where You have laid Him, and I will take Him away." Jesus said to her, "Mary!" She turned and said to Him, "Rabboni!" (which is to say, Teacher). Jesus said to her, "Do not cling to Me, for I have not yet ascended to My Father; but go to My brethren and say to them, 'I am ascending to My Father and your Father, and to My God and your God.' " Mary Magdalene came and told the disciples that she had seen the Lord, and that He had spoken these things to her.

Just as we read in the book of Genesis, there was a man, a woman, and God in the Garden of Eden. So do we have the same setting here—a man, a woman, and the presence of God in this garden? Was satan here in this garden like he was in Eden? By all means yes, yes, yes! Indwelling in and about to strike through Mary! That old and wicked, no good, low life, filthy, deceiving serpent knew if he could get to the resurrected Christ before He had ascended to the Father, he would have us in a death grip again! What does God do to ensure His plan is not fouled up in "this garden?" God has positioned two angels in the tomb, one at the head and one at the feet of where Jesus has lain. Now why do we not have the angels present at the time the disciples came back to the tomb with Mary? Why? Because they were not needed then! They were needed when Mary, with all of her whining and crying, mourning and weeping, was about to lay her hands on Jesus Christ. This is the exact same way Eve was used by the devil to lay her hands on Adam, and so began the process of our losing it all! But wait! Who could these angels be? Were they just a couple of ministering angels, or could they have been the cherubim we left with flaming swords back in the Garden of Eden? Were these those powerful ones commissioned by God to assist our God in this eternal moment of victory?! God was not going to allow satan to get within a millimeter of maneuvering a power move on His Son at this time, without God being assured that Jesus had backup!

Getting back to Mary Magdalene. Mary is totally ignorant of the enemy's deceptive plot to use her as his conduit. Therefore, let's not try to glorify Mary's weeping and mourning, O.K.? Our enemy, satan, and his demonic forces are wicked and cunning. This is the same Mary out of whom Jesus cast seven demons in Luke 8:2. If satan had possession of her before, he certainly had access to use her now. What better time than while she is in a state of mourning? She, unlike us today, did not have the indwelling of the Holy Spirit to stand against the wiles of the wicked one. We have no idea what type of vain imaginations Mary may have had about the Lord. Yes, we know she loved Him, but let's get real. Our love for people who are holy does not necessarily mean the emotions we feel for them are holy! I also think it would be wise to note that satan had schemed and planned to stop at nothing in making a last ditch attempt to get to Jesus. Furthermore, without the indwelling of the Holy Spirit, at that time, she also had no catalyst to stop her from being used of satan.

The angels ask her why she's weeping (verse 13). She says, "They've taken My Lord . . . ." Next she hears the man she thinks is the gardener ask her the same question about why she's weeping and who is it she is seeking (verse 15). She responds to the would be gardener, "Give Him to me, I'll take Him away!" Now I ask you, where in all of God's green earth was she going to go with an approximate 200 pound corpse? How was she going to drag Him outta' there? Had she been working out and had bulked up? What, pray tell, was she going to do with the corpse if she got hold of it? I'll say it again; the evil, wicked one was behind the scene on this one! But all praises to Our God! This is the clincher! This mystery has been here all the time waiting to be unlocked!

In verse 16 Mary finally realizes it is Jesus, and with this startling discovery she (unknown that the enemy is using her) is about to make her move. Verse 17, Jesus makes an imperative statement, a command to Mary. He says to her don't cling to Me (NKJV). In the original King James Version it reads don't touch Me. When looking up the word *touch* in the *Strong's Concordance*, it is listed number 680 and number 681:

> *New Testament (NT):680*
> *haptomai (hap'-tom-ahee); reflexive of NT:681; properly, to attach oneself to, i.e. to touch (in many implied relations):*
> *KJV - touch.*

> *NT:681*
> *hapto (hap'-to); a primary verb; properly, to fasten to, i.e. (specially) to set on fire:*
> *KJV - kindle, light.*

Now do we clearly see what the many definitions of touch are? To attach oneself, to touch, to fasten, to set on fire, to kindle and light! What was the enemy about to do? The enemy would have Mary touch Jesus in such a way it may have caused a sexual fire to be ignited in Him. Now in the times past there were probably many times Mary lovingly touched Him, for they fellowshipped often, yet in no way inappropriate. But this time Jesus sees something's up and is not ignorant of satan's devices (2 Corinthians 2:11) and concludes it is satan, not Mary who is after Him! Again, it is satan, not Mary who is after Him! Our Lord, who had just defeated death, hell and the grave, is discerning enough to spot the enemy's wicked plan. He would not even allow Mary to touch Him at all! Why? Was this not the same touch satan seduced Eve into making with Adam?

Let's revisit that scripture again in Genesis 3:3, where Eve is reciting God's command to them, "You shall not eat it, nor shall you touch it, lest you die." That touch in the *Strong's Concordance* is listed 5060 (Hebrew). This word touch means:

> *naga` (naw-gah'); a primitive root; properly, to touch, i.e. lay the hand upon (for any purpose; euphem.,* **to lie with a woman***); by implication, to reach (figuratively, to arrive, acquire); violently,*

to strike (punish, defeat, destroy, etc.):

Jesus knew all too well that satan seduced the man and woman in the Garden of Eden the first time. Jesus was not going to allow satan to get to Him through this woman, in the secret early morning hours, this time. It would have cost Him everything He had been so obedient to accomplish . . . it would have cost everything! All that had been both defeated and conquered would probably have suffered loss. It was not a mystery to satan, that once Jesus ascended to heaven, that was it! It would be over for satan for good. The devil gets no revelation from God, but when God's revelation is revealed and released into the earth, the devil certainly knows what it means and what it has the power to accomplish.

So what happens next? With that same power and authority Jesus had used to heal the sick, to cast out demons, and to raise the dead, He used that same authority when commanding Mary. He used that same power as He withstood the forces of the enemy. In other words He said to Mary, "You have all this excitement inside of you. Right now you are filled with mixed emotions over the idea that I am alive and not dead so go and release that zeal by preaching the good news to My brethren. Declare to them I have risen and now ascend to my Father!"

It is so wonderful to watch God outfox the enemy for good! Jesus got total victory over any and every sexual temptation (Hebrews 4:14-16) and we likewise must do the same! We are more than conquerors and He causes us to triumph in each and every situation!

Now let us turn our attention to the new baby church that has to begin to walk out these principles of God according to His plan.

Strong With No Failure To Thrive

JUST AS IT IS in the natural with a newborn baby, so it is in the spiritually newborn baby church. In the natural, we place no demands on a newborn infant other than our desires to see him with a healthy appetite, and a warm response to our love and affection. Well the leadership of the church did not want the new baby Gentiles to become discouraged with too many rules and regulations. What they did was to set in place the minimum requirements expected of new converts. We read these in Acts 15: 19-20:

> *Therefore I judge that we should not trouble those from among the Gentiles who are turning to God, but that we write to them to abstain from things polluted by idols, from sexual immorality, from things strangled, and from blood.*

This was then ratified and settled as recorded in Acts 21: 25. The leadership had to be aware there is a close connection to idolatrous worship and sexual immorality. If any believer in Christ is going to be tempted by the devil, especially new converts, these would be the areas of greatest temptation. After all, when we reflect back to the first called out "quasi-church," if you will, it was the group left to themselves for forty days and forty nights without Moses' eagle eye that blew it. When they rose up to play, they did it in connection with the worship of the golden calf (I Corinthians 10: 7-8).

It is virtually impossible to say a Christian can be involved in wanton sexual misconduct, and at the same time experience great passion for the Lord. No way! At the base of all gross sexual misconduct is a heart drawn after another god. Many times the person is unaware of this. We know, a person must be deceived on some level to a greater or lesser degree in order to be drawn away and enticed.

After coming to this point in your reading, you should be asking yourself if there are any areas in your life where you are in error. If you are not sure, ask the Lord to reveal to you hidden areas of which you may be unaware. If we would do the least bit of introspection with the help of the Holy Spirit, we would be amazed at the "hidden sins" we have been tolerating in our Christian walk. Some of them are our own little strongholds we refuse to talk about with our Father in heaven. Oh, but what a loving Father He is and is patiently waiting for us to come to Him with repentant hearts and a desire for help. He alone can bring us through.

As we begin to look at New Testament scriptures regarding the position we should take as "the overcoming church," we need to be mindful of the need to make some behavioral changes and get delivered from old mindsets. We can ill afford the costly luxury of playing ignorant. Ignorance has cost the church far too much already. Hosea 4:6a says:

My people are destroyed for lack of knowledge.

We each need to take a good look at ourselves and believe that Our God, who is faithful, will bring us to sexual health and wholeness. What we need to take an honest look at first, however, is the fact that we are constantly being tempted by one thing and then another. We are tempted on every hand, yet, I put it to you, these temptations Jesus had to endure and be victorious over, during his brief three and a half year ministry, had to be many times more powerful than what we are faced with on a regular basis. For far too long we have had our own perceptions of how Jesus' encounters with the enemy must have been. I think we tend to do this because we don't want to look at the total debauchery and depravity of mankind. To really look at our passions and our out-of-control appetites is to begin to understand how great a victory Jesus had to win to bring us back to oneness with the Father! One man had to bridge an entire lost and dying world back into right standing with God. What a massive undertaking! This should behoove each of us to truly pray and cry out to the living God, who gives much mercy and grace to help in a time of need.

> *Seeing then that we have a great High Priest who has passed through the heavens, Jesus the Son of God, let us hold fast our confession. For we do not have a High Priest who cannot sympathize with our weaknesses, but was in all points tempted as we are, yet without sin. Let us therefore come boldly to the throne of grace, that we may obtain mercy and find grace to help in time of need. Hebrews 4:14-16*

When we reflect on His encounter with Mary in the garden, we know at this point Jesus was a mighty, conquering champion.

Eye Of An Eagle

PAUL IS RESPONDING TO the early church at Corinth in his first letter to them about issues regarding sexual behaviors. As we addressed in a previous chapter, Paul makes a blanket statement in the first verse of chapter 7. It is good for a man not to touch a woman." (1 Corinthians 7:1b). Now again I ask you, why would Paul write that? Even though Paul himself lived a celibate lifestyle, we simply looked at this as Paul's own plan of "managed care" for the sin nature he may have wrestled with. We have no scriptural evidence of Paul having any temptations of a sexual nature, but we do know he had to confront and overcome areas that challenged his flesh. We read about these in Rom. 7:15-24:

> *For what I am doing, I do not understand. For what I will to do, that I do not practice; but what I hate, that I do. If, then, I do what I will not to do, I agree with the law that it is good. But now, it is no longer I who do it, but sin that dwells in me. For I know that in me (that is, in my flesh) nothing good dwells; for to will is present with me, but how to perform what is good I do not find. For the good that I will to do, I do not do; but the evil I will not to do, that I practice. Now if I do what I will not to do, it is no longer I who do it, but sin that dwells in me. I find then a law, that evil is present with me, the one who wills to do good. For I delight in the law of God according to the inward man. But I see another law in my members, warring against the law of my mind, and bringing me into captivity to the law of sin which is in my members. O wretched man that I am! Who will deliver me from this body of death?*

Paul, commissioned by God with apostolic oversight, sees that it is necessary to write to the church at Corinth. He certainly has the Father's insight on many important issues of the day as they pertain to the church. Paul knows that the new converts are full of zeal and excitement in Christ, but he also knows it is important to address the level of immaturity in the many areas of their lives, with regard to their newly adopted Christian lifestyle. Paul is doing back then, what should still be done on a large scale today, and that is to address these issues of immoral behavior more candidly. We are far too hush-hush in the church today. God knew, in His infinite wisdom and knowledge, that at the base of man's every fleshly desire was a tendency toward immorality; so He had to devise a way to moralize his nature. Hence, God instituted rules and regulations (the law), and set these as boundaries by which man would govern these tendencies. Let's take a look at David and the showbread in regard to this issue of not touching a woman. We read in 1 Samuel 21:1-5:

> Now David came to Nob, to Ahimelech the priest. And Ahimelech was afraid when he met David, and said to him, "Why are you alone, and no one is with you?" So David said to Ahimelech the priest, "The king has ordered me on some business, and said to me, 'Do not let anyone know anything about the business on which I send you, or what I have commanded you.' And I have directed my young men to such and such a place. Now therefore, what have you on hand? Give me five loaves of bread in my hand, or whatever can be found." And the priest answered David and said, "There is no common bread on hand; but there is holy bread, if the young men have at least kept themselves from women." Then David answered the priest, and said to him, "Truly, women have been kept from us about three days since I came out. And the vessels of the young men are holy, and the bread is in effect common, even though it was sanctified in the vessel this day."

Most of the time we are under the impression that it is the things in the church that are far more holy than "those things inside of us." We must never forget that the church is us and we are the church. We see clearly by this Old Testament example that the men not being with women was of paramount importance to the priest when he conferred with David. At this point in time the sacred emblems of the temple were more holy than the people, but not so today. Jesus lives on the inside of us; therefore, it is imperative we become a true temple of holiness.

Will Real Men Please Stand Up

THE ISSUE OF SEXUAL immorality is one of the biggest areas to tackle in the church. 1 Corinthians 7:2 says let each man have his own wife and each wife her husband. Young adults need to be getting married by the droves today like never before, if they have a need to be sexually fulfilled. These free swinging singles, with all their running around having sex with everything not nailed down, are bringing such a stench before the nostrils of God. This must stop! 1 Timothy 4:1-3 says:

> Now the Spirit expressly says that in latter times some will depart from the faith, giving heed to deceiving spirits and doctrines of demons, speaking lies in hypocrisy, having their own conscience seared with a hot iron, forbidding to marry, and commanding to abstain from foods which God created to be received with thanksgiving by those who believe and know the truth.

Men, you Christian men, ought to be ashamed of yourselves! If you are sexually active, single, and call yourself a Christian, it is imperative you begin to pray and seek the Lord as you start thinking in terms of a wife. Again, there is no doubt that satan is behind this wicked scheme that is causing an ever increasing minimum number of marriages in the church, and a maximum number of out-of-wedlock babies being born, or Christian women aborting the seed of tomorrow. This must stop now! Men, get serious and get a wife. If she is good enough to fulfill your every sexual desire on call, she is good enough to marry. Perhaps you are wondering why I specifically address the men and hold them accountable for the low numbers of marriages. I am still from the old school when thinking in terms of how an engagement comes about. I believe the marriage proposal should come from the man. God has created men to be the pursuers and to do the chasing. God made men to naturally be aggressive in that way. Unfortunately, with the new attitude of the supposedly "more liberal" woman of today, men do not get much opportunity to do what is supposed to come natural to them. The Bible says in Proverbs 18:22:

> *He who finds a wife finds a good thing,*
> *And obtains favor from the LORD.*

Now there are exceptions to every rule. I know there are perhaps many testimonies of women who have proposed to men and it was met with an enthusiastic response by the man; but again, I believe those are the exceptions.

Getting back to the baby church and how it addressed many of the concerns of the day regarding sexual behaviors. If we note Paul's terminology and his possible line of thought, we see in 1 Corinthians 7:6 he specifies that what he previously mentioned in 1 Corinthians 7:1-5 was not spoken by him as a commandment, but he said it by concession:

> *Now concerning the things of which you wrote to me: It is good for a man not to touch a woman. Nevertheless, because of sexual immorality, let each man have his own wife, and let each woman have her own husband. Let the husband render to his wife the affection due her, and likewise also the wife to her husband. The wife does not have authority over her own body, but the husband does. And likewise the husband does not have authority over his own body, but the wife does. Do not deprive one another except with consent for a time, that you may give yourselves to fasting and prayer; and come together again so that [s]atan does not tempt you because of your lack of self-control. But I say this as a concession, not as a commandment.*

This is not an area where spouses are to be browbeaten with regard to this issue, or have harsh demands made of them with regard to sex. By the same token, we do not want to withhold sex from one another as an act of punishment toward our spouse. Paul, who walked in a celibate lifestyle, wanted it to be understood that there are those occasions when one or the other mate may feel lead of the spirit to fast and seek the Lord, perhaps over issues on his or her mind. These issues do not necessarily have to be issues of a personal nature. There can be an unction to fast for a myriad of spiritual reasons. One may want to fast and pray over unsaved family members, getting clarity about a particular scripture, over a decision that needs to be made, etc. We need to have a more understanding heart in this area, even though it is typically an area where more debates than a few arise, but Jesus said this in Matthew 9:14–15 in response to John's disciples inquiry about this issue:

> *Then the disciples of John came to Him, saying, "Why do we and the Pharisees fast often, but Your disciples do not fast?" And Jesus said to them, "Can the friends of the bridegroom mourn as long as the bridegroom is with them? But the days will come when the bridegroom will be taken away from them, and then they will fast."*

We have not come to the place of having a high regard for fasting and prayer as a part of S.O.P. (Standard Operating Procedure) in the church in America. Perhaps there is a greater sense of the need for fasting and prayer among the peoples of other countries around the world, but we in America have not viewed fasting and prayer as strongly as we should. Fasting and prayer is a great catalyst for a person understanding who he or she is as a person, and clearly seeing those idiosyncrasies that flaw the personality and character.

Fasting and prayer has the great ability to cause keener awareness of one's sense of power and control, or lack thereof, in areas where weaknesses tend to be. We very well know, according to the scriptures, that Jesus Christ will return for a church unblemished. Looking at the church today, we wonder how and when this will ever be. I believe we are the hold-up and the biggest hindrance to the return of Jesus Christ. I also believe the area of sexual immorality is the number one problem for the church. The church has many, many issues to work on and work through; yet, in regard to sexual impropriety the state of affairs in the church is a major universal problem.

A Chance Meeting

A most surprising thing occurred in the summer of 2000. While I was in the midst of writing this book I traveled to the Caribbean. On the last Saturday of the month I was there, the ministry team was to assemble in the lobby of the hotel early that morning, and wait for our transportation to the airport because it was time to head home. I was the first person downstairs that morning and as I looked around to see if there were others in the lobby, I spotted a young married man to whom I had the privilege of ministering to on the previous Friday night. He rushed over and gave me a hug and told me how blessed he and his wife were with the prophetic word I had given to them. He proceeded to tell me how they were already in the midst of fulfilling some of what I had said to them. He spoke of his ministry he has to men, and particularly to minister to married men. He began to speak of an area that seemed to really burden his heart . . . it was sexual promiscuity. He said, "I really hate to see men mistreating their wives and being unfaithful to them. It is a real problem here. Don't get me wrong," he went on to say, "I know it is a problem in the entire Body of Christ, but it is very, very, bad here with the men in the church. They don't seem to understand how much they are hurting their wives." Well, needless to say, I was in seventh heaven! I had been asking the Lord while I was there if this was a real problem in their country as well, or was this just really bad in the good ole' U.S.A.? God certainly knows how to get the "411" (information) to His people!

The conversation I had with this particular brother, was just one of many. Since I started writing this book I have had so many conversations with people about sexual issues—especially about many perversions people are shackled with. We know nothing in the kingdom of God happens by chance. I have to believe God ordained these different people to speak with me about the personal challenges they were facing, because God wanted me to know for sure that this is a very real issue in the church. What's even more surprising is that every one of those conversations that came about were all unsolicited!

As I reflect over what I have presented so far, in terms of the written material, I am very aware of the fact I have attempted to cover a broad range of topics. We have looked at the fall in the Garden of Eden, Old and New Testament examples of sexual conduct, the importance of fasting and prayer, satan's last attempt to get to Jesus Christ, and the need for us to raise the standard, by improving our behavior as Christians around the issues of sex. It is necessary, however, that we again focus our attention on yet another very critical issue in the area of sexual impropriety that has been a great hindrance to the church for eons.

The Unmarried Virgin

T̶HERE IS A DIFFERENCE between a wife and a virgin. The unmarried woman cares about the things of the Lord, that she may be holy both in body and in spirit. But she who is married cares about the things of the world—how she may please her husband. And this I say for your own profit, not that I may put a leash on you, but for what is proper, and that you may serve the Lord without distraction. But if any man thinks he is behaving improperly toward his virgin, if she is past the flower of youth, and thus it must be, let him do what he wishes. He does not sin; let them marry. Nevertheless he who stands steadfast in his heart, having no necessity, but has power over his own will, and has so determined in his heart that he will keep his virgin, does well. So then he who gives her in marriage does well, but he who does not give her in marriage does better.

But she is happier if she remains as she is, according to my judgment--and I think I also have the Spirit of God.

1 Corinthians 7:34-38, 40

I cannot help but be reminded of the doctrine of the Essenes, which we discussed in the second chapter of the book—the whole notion of a celibate lifestyle as the ultimate lifestyle for mankind. John the Baptist and Jesus Christ were ones who espoused the principles of the Essenes with regard to their "no – sex" policy. I am sure there are many liberated Christian and non-Christian women alike, who would say this passage of scripture is out of the dark ages. For many a young woman in America, there would be absolutely no way in this 21st century she would await the consent of her father to determine whether or not she could marry. Much of society would say the father was being emotionally abusive to do such a cruel thing to his daughter.

I, for one, am very much in favor of young women being as free to dream, explore, and experience life just as our young men are allowed. With all the exploring and discovering, however, there is never a need for promiscuous behavior on the part of males or females.

It never ceases to amaze me how young men want to marry "nice" girls, but they also want to have much opportunity to sow their wild oats and have a whole bunch of dry runs with someone's daughter, while they are waiting to find Miss Right. For the most part, all Miss Rights would like to also have someone they could call their own, but it is so surprising how many young women will say they don't want a husband without experience. This "learn together" philosophy regarding sexual relations can stir up quite a dilemma in the hearts of young ladies in waiting.

In getting a clear understanding of what Paul was talking about in First Corinthians, we see it lines up with the Heavenly Father having the final authority to say when the Bride, the church, will be ready for the Bridegroom, Jesus Christ. If more single females understood the blessedness of the spiritual transfer of authority from her father to the would-be-husband on her wedding day, she would not squawk and resist so much.

We saw this practice often in the Catholic Church in past decades. Thousands and thousands of single females were sent away to the convent, so as to embrace a married life with Christ as opposed to becoming married to an adoring young guy she perhaps had begun to love from afar. According to the above scriptures, her father was well within his rights to exercise his liberty in this area. It also goes without saying that these young women were many times already studying in a convent or attending an all girls' school. This major decision was being made long before she was older in years, or had already had a taste of a free single lifestyle. These women usually went right from under the authority of dad to the authority of the convent. Today I encourage the young, single women of our church to stay at home with parents until it is time to get married. It is so much easier especially for a daughter to stay in the home and submit to her parent's watchful care, than to be out in her own place, doing her own thing, and then many times find herself years down the road, unhappy, lonely and in a ton of debt to boot. Some single women have moved out on their own and have done very well in keeping their focus on their careers or school. They even kept dating in the proper perspective until the eventful wedding day, but it is usually rare to see this.

Now there are two points I want to look at with regard to these scriptures. In verse 38 we see that Paul says a father does well to give his daughter in marriage, but he also states the father who doesn't give his daughter does better. This statement is in keeping with the line of thinking I have been trying to establish since we started this book . . . the celibate lifestyle that John the Baptist lived, that Jesus Christ lived, that Paul eventually took on, is the same lifestyle the young lady would experience if she were to embrace her father's wishes for her. Paul writes in such a way to point out that this is by no means a lesser plan—as if it appears to be the option for those that would have otherwise failed in the affairs of the heart. We in the church must understand that there will be those who will gladly choose to adopt a celibate lifestyle, will have "grace" from God for it and will love it. We cannot continue to say there is something wrong with men and women who, for whatever reason, choose a celibate lifestyle. For them it is viewed as the only normal thing to do. Jesus points this out in Matt. 19:12:

> *For there are eunuchs who were born thus from their mother's womb, and there are eunuchs who were made eunuchs by men, and there are eunuchs who have made themselves eunuchs for the kingdom of heaven's sake. He who is able to accept it, let him accept it.*

Today, as well as at the time Jesus spoke this truth, eunuchs are very much alive on planet earth. These are persons like Mother Theresa. They serve God their entire life with no thought or desire of ever being sexually involved. This is called a celibate lifestyle. What many single people are attempting to do, with any convictions at all, is walk in an abstinent lifestyle. This is when a person purposes to take control of the desires of the flesh, and refuses to be sexually involved until marriage. When one takes on the abstinent lifestyle as an option, there needs to be a clear understanding that it is with the knowledge that no provisions are made to satisfy the lusts and longings of the flesh. In reading 1 Corinthians 7:34 we must truly emphasize the point of one being " . . . holy both in body and in spirit."

Part Four

And the end of all our exploring
will be to arrive where we started
and know the place for the first time.
—T.S. Eliot
Four Quartets

A Dialogue On The Issue Of Masturbation

PERHAPS SOME OF YOU reading this book may be aware of a monumental problem in the church that most of the church has ignored for far too long, the problem of masturbation. This has become, unfortunately, the alternative to having sexual intercourse outside of marriage, the alternative for unfulfilled married partners, or an alternate route for those who plan to remain single. None of the above is approved by God. Will masturbation mean we will be banished to hell? No. What it does mean, however, is there is a part of the person's being, on this side of glory, that can never experience God in the fullness He would want for that individual. I believe that the issue of masturbation, if addressed now at the dawning of the 21st century church, is dealt with head-on, we can overcome a deluge of spiritual tragedy that could come upon the church in the times ahead.

I was so excited when I returned home from the Caribbean, to find that one of my friends in the ministry had done quite a bit of research on this topic for me. It was such a gift from God to get home and find that she had been led by the Holy Spirit to check out this topic in such detail. What follows is a conversation she and I had with regard to the subject of masturbation. I decided to address this issue in a dialogue format, and it is my hope this will prove both interesting and thought provoking.

Pastor B: Well, Kim, why were you interested in looking into the area of masturbation?

Kim: To be quite truthful about this, and I don't know if I want you to print this Pastor Barbara, but, to be quite honest, because of the different things I had experienced when I was married to my late husband. He wasn't able to . . . we weren't able to have sexual relations because of his M.S. (Multiple Sclerosis). There came a point in our marriage when we started going to an agency that helps people facing this challenge. We spoke with their counselors on the subject of how the caregiver, the spouse that would be giving the care, how she was to have her sexual needs met. One of the things available is an Internet site which provides feedback from different people who face similar challenges. I remember reading a comment from a caregiver, a wife who wrote that she nurtures her husband, she builds his self-esteem, but since they cannot have relations, she recommended masturbating. I had a problem with that because I didn't believe in it, and I had been taught in the church that it is not acceptable to the Lord; but at the same time I was having negative feelings about not having my sexual needs met at all. So I had a counseling session one day with you, Pastor Barbara, and one of the things that came out during that counseling session was the whole notion of self-gratification and the exalting of self. As you began to write this book, one day the Lord just started dealing with me. I had some questions in my mind and I went on the Internet one night looking for answers. I found a lot of information about masturbating in general. I think I even told you that one of the denominational church organizations have had a site on the Internet devoted to how to stop masturbating. As I looked into that, the Lord revealed to me one of the root causes of masturbation. He led me to a study that began with the Caananite gods and how people worshipped such gods during that time. One study led to another and here we are.

Pastor B: It is unfortunate that masturbation is what the world offers as a solution to partners when it seems that all else is not going to work out for physical needs to be met. This really puts many Christians and non-Christians alike in a catch-22 depending on their own personal views about sex and the issue of masturbation. On the one hand they may want to be faithful and fully committed to enjoying sex in a healthy and fulfilling manner, but on the other hand if they buy into the "if it feels good to you, do it" ploy, they find themselves trying to stave off the onslaught of guilt and/or shame that is sure to overtake them at the conclusion of their moment of ecstasy. I can say for myself, being that I came of age after the 50's and 60's, in thinking back to those years, the whole issue of masturbation was quite taboo. Many people from the baby boomer generation had the same feelings as myself, so I can't believe that everybody is all of a sudden O.K. with this. There were a lot of problems with people feeling that it was O.K., even if they engaged in it, they didn't necessarily think it was morally right. You know, Kim, as you spoke and talked about self-gratification it just caused me to think about the word narcissism. There is a mythological story regarding a youth who fell in love with his own image reflected in a pool, and then he wasted away from unsatisfied desire. Whereupon, he was transformed into the flower which we today know as the Narcissus. Narcissistic behavior is actually considered erotic gratification derived from admiration of one's own physical or mental attributes. I learned in the church, about 20 years ago, that the whole notion of being able to gratify one's self does not leave room for the body to be satisfied or gratified by the man or the woman that is to be one's mate.

There are two schools of thought for me. I am liberal enough in my thinking to feel that as a woman, women should be in touch with their bodies enough to know their erogenous zones and what brings them pleasure from head to toe. This, a woman should certainly be able to communicate to her husband. However, I have a problem with a woman just gratifying herself in those pleasurable areas without the need of her husband's involvement. I don't see her self-gratification in this way as being normal.

What other thoughts would you like to share based on your own experiences?

Kim: In that the act of masturbating is usually something that is done in secret, one of the things that happens, is a person turns all his attention to himself in gratifying his own desires. Those who masturbate totally remove the possibility of anyone else coming in and doing that for them, namely their spouse. Unfortunately, they may become accustomed only to their own touch. I know one of the things which should be a signal that masturbation is not pleasing to the Lord, is when a person walks away with a feeling of guilt and or shame; that feeling of being dirty and incomplete. Even with what the wife was saying on the Internet, I could tell from her writing that there was still a longing for her husband. And even with myself, if I were to have engaged in masturbation, it was not going to take away the fact that I wanted to be intimate with my husband.

The sort of intimacy with one's mate, you do not reach when you are getting your jollies by yourself because the intimacy isn't there—it's just a physical thing. The level of intimacy, what God intended in lovemaking and its fulfillment, isn't there.

Pastor B: Well you know in part of the research that you shared with me you made an interesting statement. You say, "Masturbation is a secret act under a shade tree (an act in and of darkness), with a wooden image (interpretation—whatever is stirring the ungodly imagination to incite the sexual act). The worst part is that it is a seducing lie from the enemy, 'you are not doing anything against the Lord, it's just you.' It isn't just you, however, it is in His sanctuary, your body; and for a child of the Lord, a part of His bride, it is adulterous."

Now Kim, that brings to mind the scripture in 1 Corinthians 6:18-20 where Paul states:

> *Flee sexual immorality. Every sin that a man does is outside the body, but he who commits sexual immorality sins against his own body. Or do you not know that your body is the temple of the Holy Spirit who is in you, whom you have from God, and you are not your own? For you were bought at a price; therefore glorify God in your body and in your spirit, which are God's.*

So just based on what you said makes me think that this whole idea of a secret act under a shade tree, and an act done in darkness means God does not want us to do those kinds of things. He wants us to be very aware of the fact that our physical bodies have been carved out as a warehouse to allow Him to cohabitate with us. He wants to create within this physical body a sanctuary of His own. Subsequently, this reflects what Paul spoke of in 1 Corinthians 6. So, Kim, where does the whole idea about the shade tree come in?

Kim: One of the things that I uncovered in my research was that the Phoenician people, the Caananites, and other groups that the children of Israel were to dispossess, served many pagan gods. As part of their pagan worship, there was the worship of Baal, and the worship of Ashtoreth (Ashtoreth being the female counterpart of Baal) and in worship of those gods, the pagan people did a lot of sacrificing. One part of the sacrificing was that they sacrificed themselves. They sacrificed their children, but they also sacrificed or gave their bodies to unholy and perverse sexual practices. Not only did they engage in sex with the temple prostitutes, but they engaged in sex with the actual objects, the Ashtoreth and Baal objects, some of which were made in the form of animals. Some were made in the form of human figures, and some of them were made in the form of other natural elements. The shaded areas refer to the fact that when the pagan people, and even when the children of Israel became involved in all of the idolatry, they built shrines to their gods in the high places. In worshipping them and giving their bodies to them, they were in shaded places—hidden places, places underneath the trees, in crevices, and in caves. The groves refer to the wood from which the Asheroths were made. In 1 Kings 14:23 of *Today's English Version* of the Bible, it reads, "They built places of worship for false gods and put up stone pillars and symbols of Asherah to worship on the hills and under shady trees."

This is what the Bible refers to when the Lord condemns the children of Israel for what they were doing with the groves in the shaded places. They were not only worshipping these gods, but they were also doing perverse things with them.

Pastor B: I try to make a point in the book that there is a close tie between sexual immorality (and all kinds of sexual sin people get into) and idolatry. On the surface we don't think about idolatry being tied to sexual sin and most certainly we don't see ourselves committing idolatry when we engage in masturbation. However, if we truly understand the scripture, we are. In the book of Corinthians it says " . . . our bodies are the temple of the Holy Spirit." So what one really does is get into a kind of adulterous act. Even more interesting to me is the idea which you shared about the trees. In the beginning when God created man, there was a tree in the Garden of Eden that God told Adam not to touch. There was a tree of good and evil and a tree of life. We see that trees are very, very significant to God, the Almighty God whom we serve. So now you can see how the enemy in his own slickness and perverseness is also going to put great emphasis on the use of trees, whether it's the whole grove of trees or specific trees, or to have people enter into idolatrous worship with him by committing these perverse acts in, under, and around trees.

Today, especially here in the U.S.A., people are certainly not entertaining the idea of consciously going up to trees to commit some perverse act as they did in former times; but by the same token we are people given to doing a lot of inappropriate things with all kinds of sexual tools and toys that are the by-products of trees. We have to remember that even God refers to us as "trees of righteousness." If we in the privacy of our own homes and the privacy of our bedrooms, with the blinds closed, are causing this "tree of righteousness" to enter into a lewd act by ourselves, prompted by desires we seem to have no control over, it causes this "righteous tree" to enter into an act that has to bring satan a lot of satisfaction. When Christians are so weak-willed and weak-minded regarding their sexual appetites, this only feeds into the plan of satan. He wants to keep us functioning at a level where we are unable to put any stops on ourselves so that he can constantly have an opportunity to "have at us." This creates such a bad situation for Christians. This brings to mind many other things from a historical standpoint regarding Ashtoreth, Baal, and the worship of those gods. We have all read the names of those gods in the Old Testament, but we never stopped to think about how those gods were tied so closely to sexual immorality. This also reminds me of a personal situation regarding women, to whom I have had to minister deliverance in years past. One of the problems that is way out of hand with women and masturbation are the objects they use.

Kim: That is exactly what I was thinking as you were talking.

Pastor B: Yes, it may not be the Ashtoreth gods, so to speak, but there are so many items that are being used. When I did deliverance prayer with single women who wanted to get control and authority over their bodies so that they would not be constantly tempted to fornicate with men, these same women were given to the use of sexual objects as a substitute for being with a man. Both are wrong. When it comes to deliverance from masturbating I have ministered to both single and married women who were very much attached to the use of cucumbers, salami, hot dogs, hairbrush handles, soft drink bottles, and even items they go to the porno shops to purchase. Instead of the women learning to pray and ask God to help them get authority over their bodies, they would constantly give in to the use of these items. I understand now that women will even have their boyfriends or dates use these items on them as well. From your research, do you think this behavior is directly tied to the initial worship of Ashtoreth and those carved out images?

Kim: In a sense, yes. One of the reasons, and one of the tell-tale signs of this is that these images and objects become sacred to them in that they do not want anybody to know they are using them or to know anything about them. They are special and to be kept hidden. Their use is completely done in private, and this is exactly what was going on in those shaded groves. The ancient pagan worshippers might also have been doing those things in the groves because they were trying to have children or they wanted their crops to increase. Remember Ashtoreth and Baal were the gods of fertility —which they believed would bring an increase of wealth, an increase of produce, or whatever was going to cause there to be a multiplication. Today, people are using the objects solely to fulfill a need for their own sexual gratification, which in a sense is a multiplication of just their own desires. You keep doing it and doing it. Then it becomes an addiction.

Pastor B: Yes, that is one thing I have found out in talking with the women to whom I prayed with and to whom I have ministered. Once the masturbation started, there was a need to do it more and more frequently. It wasn't that they did it one time and then said to themselves, "O.K., this will keep me together for the next six months." In their mind there was this silent prayer, or prayerful thought, or a plea of "Oh God, I wish I could stop," but there was just no stopping. It just continued to increase and increase. I really understand what you are saying about the multiplicity. This makes masturbation get totally out of hand once it is started.

Kim: Yes, because it is subject to the same law of reaping and sowing. You reap it, you reap it, and you keep reaping it. When I was researching on the Internet, I found a gross thing. There was a survey of the number of people who masturbate, and a breakdown of the type of people who filled out this survey. The youngest participant was twelve years old. That was very disturbing for me to see the frequency even for twelve-year-olds, when they first started and how often they did this. For females the average was five or six times a week, for males it was five or six times a day.

Pastor B: Again in our society we have a different set of rules for men versus women. We tend to look at women engaging in masturbation with a non-consenting attitude as opposed to men doing so. Fathers even seemed to think it was O.K. for their sons to masturbate, so much so that they would talk with them and tell them that masturbation was the way to keep off tension and added pressure. I recall a situation in my teenage high school years, when a teenage boy told me that his father purchased "girlie" magazines to keep in the bathroom for his sons; this was so they could both stimulate and relieve themselves when they came home from school. There always seemed to be a different attitude parents had with sons regarding masturbation—more accepting than with their daughters. Do you have any personal thoughts on that issue Kim?

Kim: I don't know why there is such a different attitude with males over this issue versus females; however, I did read an interesting point in a medical science article. The article said men, because they produce a certain amount of sperm, naturally have nocturnal emissions; but that is not masturbation. They have nocturnal emissions period; so the body is automatically going to relieve the pent-up tension they may have. It's not necessary that they resort to looking at magazines. When a Christian becomes involved in pornography, it takes him into another class of blatant sin. Jesus said if you look on any woman to lust after her, whether she's walking down the street (or in a magazine) you have committed adultery with her.

Pastor B: Right, because everything with Christians goes back to issues of the heart. Even if you think in terms of pornography, whether it is magazines or videos, whatever people look at to stimulate themselves, I would think there has to be something on which people focus, even with masturbation people don't draw a total mental blank slate. They have to focus on something. Human beings don't become lobotomized so they can proceed with masturbation off in an ozone somewhere with no actualizing of thoughts or feelings. This discussion really makes me think of just how much we have to get control over this area of indiscretion and it also brings to mind Paul's charge to the church in 2 Corinthians 10:5:

> *Casting down arguments and every high thing that exalts itself against the knowledge of God, bringing every thought into captivity to the obedience of Christ.*

So we can readily see that we have to bring under our control every thought and every wild and vain imagination so that these things do not control us. When we think of vain imaginations it certainly gets us into the whole issue of fantasy. Many people think fantasy is O.K., but the end result is that people will fantasize about other people, other relationships, and all kinds of things that are not good. Now we know a healthy imagination is good. I can remember as a child I had a very healthy imagination. All of the kids in the neighborhood played mom, dad, house, storekeeper, doctor, lawyer, and Indian Chief, and we just made up all kinds of games. So to have a healthy imagination is good, but when the imagination becomes polluted to the point that you, as a Christian, are constantly fantasizing about people you know that you cannot be with, that is bad. Even single Christian women will fantasize a great deal about married men, or many women, both married or single will fantasize about their male pastors. Men are known to fantasize about being with women, and they can be any and every type of woman. That has been an acceptable norm forever! Yet, these fantasies left unchecked will, too, eventually lead to disaster.

Now that you have recently become widowed and are still young, Kim, what are some of your thoughts about what people can do to get control over masturbation by dealing first with the fantasies of their mind?

Kim: Well, one of the things that needs to happen is dialogue. The first step is bringing the issues out. There are so many people in the church that are struggling with this masturbation issue. Since you began writing this book I have received two phone calls. One call was from someone in our church, and the other was a call from someone outside of our church. These persons said they had not engaged in masturbation, but all of a sudden they felt they were being attacked by a desire to masturbate. They had thoughts about doing this. Underlying all of this, however, was the enemy who would have prompted them to go ahead and give in to masturbating. Instead by them calling and getting this temptation out in the open, by speaking up and saying something about it, they were able to get some control. The enemy would certainly have planned to badger them in their minds, having them think they should be doing this, bringing up different people in their thoughts, bringing up longings they had inside their heart, and this would therefore, have incited them, bringing them to a place of self-gratification. So again, the first thing is to dialogue and let it be known. Say to someone, "Hey, I'm struggling in this area and really having a problem with this." The other thing to do is to reflect on the scripture you just quoted in 2 Corinthians 10. One of the things the Lord showed me is that we present our bodies as living sacrifices. Within the confines of marriage there is a covenant relationship, a covenant relationship with the man and the woman, and also a covenant relationship with the Lord. So the sexual relationship between the husband and wife, because of the covenant that is established, is actually an act of worship as they give themselves to each other in the confines of the covenant that the Lord has given to them. Masturbation, by itself, in and of itself, is sex by itself. There is no covenant and no covenant relationship in masturbation. Worship then is not going on with the Lord, but worship then is going on with one's self, and if worship is going on with one's self, by definition then, worship is going on with satan.

Pastor B: So then we do see more clearly that as worship does go on, in this case, with one's self or with satan, this brings us back to narcissistic behavior. This is unfortunate, because there are quite a few women I have talked with who do seem to think it is quite O.K., that they are abstaining from sex as they pray and wait on a husband. In the meantime they are taking care of all these pent-up physical needs with these objects that bring satisfaction so that they can (they say) maintain control. Yet, in the eyes of the Lord this person is still very much out of control. We must say clearly that every time someone masturbates, it gives the enemy more of a stronghold, more authority, and more ownership in that person's life. No wonder we have so many women up late at night on their knees pleading, begging, and crying out to God for a husband; but on the other hand, they are taking care of business with their "old stand-in" objects. Women and men cannot have their cake and eat it too! God expects all singles to make a choice and not be a fence-straddler on this issue. This very well could be part of why there is such a decline in the number of Christian marriages. Why don't the women and men think about fasting and prayer as the solution to getting control? We know fasting and prayer really helps to cleanse the mind, slay the will of the flesh, and afflict the soul. This is a necessary part of the Christian lifestyle anyway. So as you have said the dialogue is very necessary, because only when we become very candid about this issue will we understand how to begin to handle this problem. People come to church every Sunday morning nicely dressed up for God, but Monday through Saturday many of them have been off in their own "tree groves."

Again, when we talk about masturbation, many of us tend to think of this as something resigned to single males and females, but there was a situation I knew of where a married woman was ministered to by a female pastor friend of mine. She ministered to this married woman who had tremendous struggles in years gone by with all kinds of sexual promiscuity, masturbation, temptations toward male pastors, outrageous fantasies that were yanking her emotions all over the place, and it had gotten to the point it was too overwhelming for this woman to handle. Another interesting point about this middle-aged, married woman was the fact that she had become a real expert at masturbating, because she had learned to engage in it at the tender age of five—this was with experiencing orgasmic pleasure as well. This was certainly territory the enemy was not going to easily give up so this woman could go free. So, here again, this married woman was strongly considering turning back to masturbation as a tool that would help her handle emotional overload. Thanks be to God, the woman sought help from a pastor that had a tremendous anointing to bring deliverance to this woman's life. This all came about because she was willing to open up and tell someone of her struggle, just as you are suggesting.

Now, when we speak of deliverance, some people may use the term "exorcism," and I need to say that so it will bring clarity to what I am speaking of. My theology and teaching leads me to believe the term deliverance is better suited for what I am speaking of, when it pertains to people becoming free of demonic pressure or possession. Jesus Christ, as well as the prophets of old, spoke of people being delivered from oppressive powers of the enemy. This is strictly an issue of semantics as it pertains to the verbiage of choice. On last report my pastor friend said the woman she ministered to has been able to keep those thoughts out of her mind as an alternative, and is enjoying a very pleasurable sexual relationship with her husband; in other words she's getting plenty of good lovin' on a regular basis! We Christians can no longer afford to be afraid to talk about the stinkin' mess, because inevitably we end up doing the stinkin' mess! I want to also go on record by saying there are hundreds and hundreds of psychologists, therapists, social workers, counselors and the like who will say that masturbation is very healthy and therapeutic for young and old alike, and there is no problem with one taking care of their needs in this manner. This is fine for those who want to follow the ways that are contrary to the Will of God, but we Christians know there are criteria we must follow and there's just no two ways about it. As someone so aptly put it in recent years, the commandments of God are not the suggestions of God! People also need to remember that many times there is strength in numbers, and when people are faithful in attending church, becoming involved, opting to participate in support groups, or just make themselves accountable to someone who can be trusted, it can really help to eliminate the pressure. Lastly, I want to add men and women should be sexually satisfied. There should be romance and excitement over the idea of sexual satisfaction and it should all be a part of what is expected in a normal marriage.

Kim: As you were talking about the woman who was delivered, it brought to mind the need for us to know the key to the stronghold, and not just for the married partners but for single men and women as well. When a person is entertaining the idea of masturbating, it would be good for that person to stop and take a look at what is going on with him or her when the thought to masturbate comes to mind. That is usually an indication as to where the enemy has a stronghold. I will give a personal example. When I was dealing with my thoughts of masturbating, they always came about when I was frustrated about something. Usually the frustration dealt with something I didn't have a complete grasp of, or the frustration of what was going on physically with my husband and his limitations, and even what I wanted as a wife, but it always tended to be those areas. When the thought came to masturbate, the thought to go and talk about it with the Lord was not there.

Pastor B: Yes.

Kim: The thought to go and talk with the Lord was supplanted by an invasion of the enemy. At the point of satanic invasion masturbating becomes a substitute, and instead of having intimacy with God and getting my needs met there, or dealing with whatever was the cause, the ploy of the enemy was for me to have intimacy with myself.

Pastor B: Now Kim that really addresses what I came to understand about the married woman who was finally delivered. Her desires to masturbate were directly linked to the times she was feeling frustrated or upset with her husband. God, on the other hand, tells us to cast our burdens and our cares upon Him for He cares for us. Instead we often act so goofy that we are afraid to talk to God about sex. I for one am a very strong advocate of women having X-rated conversations with God about sex if needed. That is what literally carried me when I was a single female and had just come out of the world and had a very intense desire to come into a greater relationship with the Lord. One of the first areas He dealt with me was with regard to my skimpy clothes; I got rid of those and my outrageous makeup and wigs. So the Lord purposed to first talk to me about the outer. Next, He was firm on the need for me to give up sex and no longer spend time as I had with men. So here I was, at the ripe, young age of twenty-six years, in my prime, very much sexually active and suddenly I was faced with having to walk in this abstinent lifestyle for however long it was going to take. Now mind you, this was not a struggle when I first turned my life back over to the Lord. This decision to make Him Lord was in September 1976. The honeymoon period one experiences when Jesus finally becomes Lord to that person is so euphoric there is nothing else on that person's mind at the time. After a few weeks passed, however, the idea of how to date and who to date became an issue with me, not to mention how to conduct myself on a date. Actually this dating thing was not difficult for me to do because I went through the motions of doing it based solely on my ability to be a good Christian, who had made up her mind to do "good works," so I really did the right things. At that time I was very grateful for the scripture that said, "Submit to God, resist the devil, and he will flee. (James 4:7)" So literally that is what I was doing along with praying my way through and asking God to help me. At this same time in my life I had two very dear friends "on earth" to whom I made myself accountable. They were Deacons James and Barbara. They allowed me to call them whenever I needed to and would allow me to come over to their home to spend time with them, if I needed to do so. This relationship helped me tremendously, as I struggled through a very trying time. If I came up missing from Bible class or Sunday school, they would even come to my apartment. They, as well as Ruth, kept that level of depression and frustration from being overwhelming as it had been. It was very important to have them around in my "infancy stage" of walking out this new behavior. God was so good to give me friends like them. There did come a point, though, when I really started dating that God, Himself, had to tell me how to date. He showed me how to date and it was working out fine. Yet, there were those times I would come home after a date and be very stimulated in my mind, and in order for me to bring that Baal/Ashtoreth god down, I would have to have these very candid conversations with the Lord. I would say, "O.K., God, I am going to bed and I have one hand over here on the right pillow and I have the other over here on the left pillow. You come down here to my bedroom and bless my heart tonight so I can go to sleep because that brother that I just left is all I can think about right now. I don't know how in the world I am going to go to sleep, because he is not here to do anything for me and I KNOW You do not want me to do anything at all for myself . . . so come quickly Lord Jesus and help me!" Now I must say it was rather difficult for me the first time I had to do that, no one told me to do it or not to do it, I have to believe I was led of the Holy Spirit to pray in that manner. Praise be to God, He came and did just what I asked Him to do. Those desires I had to be with a man just dissipated and I went to sleep. As date after date occurred

I became even more candid in my conversations with God about what I felt, what I wanted, and what I was missing. I reminded Him of what it used to be like for me (as if He didn't know) and surprisingly enough I became stronger and stronger, date after date, and was really able to walk out the abstinent lifestyle as God was instructing me to do. I was not just strong physically, but emotionally and spiritually as I took my conversations to God and saw Him come through on each and every prayer. You are so very right, Kim, when you say we must get rid of the frustration that tends to build up in us, by talking it out with Him who most certainly knows and understands. All Christians, male and female, must learn to get rid of the strongholds the enemy will hold over our lives by getting the frustration out before God.

So Kim, as I said earlier, one of the things I did when I was single was to put my music away. That helped get rid of some of the frustration. The other thing I did was pray and talk to friends who were there for me. Unlike me, however, there is a woman in the Bible who was challenged with being frustrated and her frustration came to her differently. We have all read about her so many times. Her name is Rachel and she was married to Jacob. Your research about her was very interesting, could you share it with us?

Kim: Yes, one of the things you just talked about was the fact that you put away your music and you put away those other things that were sexually stimulating. When you said that, the Lord prompted in my mind "household gods." The scripture says that when Jacob was fleeing from Laban with Rachel, Leah, and his whole clan, Rachel took the household gods. When Laban came to search for Jacob, his family, and the stolen household gods, Laban could not find them because Rachel had put the household gods into saddle bags and was sitting on them. She told her father she could not get up for him to search, because it was the time of her monthly cycle. For Rachel these gods gave her security, they gave her pleasure and they were able to satiate her appetites. This was very distressing to Jacob and that is why he makes a demand in Genesis 35:2:

> *And Jacob said to his household and to all who were with him, "Put away the foreign gods that are among you, purify yourselves, and change your garments."*

This is the same as saying, "Get all your household gods or whatever it is that is causing you to be defiled and remove them out of your life." The thing that we have to remember is that in the home there was Jacob, Leah, the handmaids to Rachel and Leah, who are now officially concubines and mothers to his children. Rachel, therefore, knew that Jacob was not completely hers alone. This had to be very frustrating for Rachel because according to scripture, the two of them loved each other very much. This love was manifested before there was ever a wedding. Watching the man she loved go in to all these other women had to be extremely difficult for her, so she may have had it in her mind that she had to appease her appetites with her household gods just to deal with having to share her beloved. Consider the fact that she did not take the gods and bury them in the earth, which would have been very easy to do, but instead she chose to guard them by sitting on them and have them very close to a private part of her body that was considered sacred and could not be touched by a man, other than her husband. That in itself is very telling, not to mention she was still desiring to have more children and these were gods of fertility. In order for the gods to give her what she wanted, which was more children and possibly to have her husband's total devotion to her, she had to give them what they required, which was to worship them. History tells us that the worship of these pagan fertility gods included sexual and deviant behaviors, from prostitution to orgies to personal perverted worship in the groves with the wooden images.

For you it was your music that brought you pleasure, for others it may be their sexy lingerie, their scented candles or fragrances that gratifies them. Which, in effect, are objects of devotion, household gods.

Pastor B: In Genesis there are a couple of points we read about regarding the story of Rachel, Jacob, Leah and the other women, and the whole big mess with all these people. In light of the information you researched about the pagan gods, this, in turn, makes so much sense. I just want to take a minute and really look at the dynamics of this relationship in which they were all involved. In other words, "What's wrong with this picture?" Rachel was filled with despair over the fertility issue.

At the time she took the gods from her father's home, she had already birthed Joseph, yet she was very aware of the fact that Leah, and the handmaidens Bilkah and Zilpah all had more children than she; so this was still a sore spot with her. Now on top of this, you have them all planning to be this one big happy family . . . not good. See, I don't know how big the tent city was that they lived in, and how close the maid's quarters were, but I've got to believe that even in our homes, in this society, built with concrete, steel, and plaster, the sound of lovemaking has come through on many occasions. The bottom line is people have often been overheard. We have no idea of how much of this "carrying on" Rachel could hear, or did she actually see Jacob put his hand around Leah as he walked her to her private bedchamber, knowing what was about to happen? In reality it would have to have been very painful. We, as women who are given to emotion much more than men, would have a very hard time with this set-up.

All I can say is thank God I am not the one, perish the thought. I am so glad I was born today; it just would not work for me. This also brings to mind the fact that even though we are in the 21st century, there are women who suspect they are sharing their husbands with outside women. Whether in Christian or non-Christian homes, this fooling around and unfaithfulness goes on, and on a very regular basis, and it does nothing but bring pain. This in itself causes wives to resort to drastic measures, either getting into self-gratification, adultery, or addictive habits of all kinds. This, too, caused Rachel to resort to what she determined was a drastic measure—stealing the gods. Unfortunately by stealing the pagan gods and then serving the Living God, too, she was playing on both sides of the fence. We know she was critically linked to the righteous lineage out of whom Jesus would eventually come, yet she was not fully aware of how dangerous it was for her to get mixed up in idolatry and get on the enemy's playground.

Kim: Jacob was aware of this interaction with the other gods. This is why Jacob was so demanding about them having put the gods away from them. He was very angry over the idea of any lesser gods being worshipped among those of his clan.

Pastor B: Yes, he did discover this idolatry. At first Jacob didn't know about Rachel and the household gods because he told Laban to kill whomever he found to have the gods. There is no way Jacob would have given Laban permission to kill the person if he thought for one minute the person was his beloved Rachel! Just as situations like this existed back then, they exist like this today. No, we are not camped out in tents, traveling on camels, but men still get in their cars, as well as women, and they go venturing out to "do their thing,"—things that should not be done, especially for Christians. The sole purpose is just to satisfy the flesh. It should also be noted, Kim, that this issue with Rachel was a far more serious offense in the eyes of God than we have really understood. We read in Genesis 35:19 that Rachel died while giving birth to Benjamin. His name is changed to Benjamin by his father, thank goodness, because as Rachel was dying she names him Ben-Oni, which means "son of my sorrow." Why was she sorrowful? Where was her joy, after all she was no longer childless? What was she hurting over? I believe she hurt over knowing the favor of God was not upon her as it was with the others. When looking up the meaning of the city Ephrath, to which they were journeying, it means "fruitfulness." The Lord was not going to allow Rachel to come into fruitfulness in her sin . . . she would only beget more sin! If they were all about to come into a fruitful place in God, it was certainly going to be a time of abundant harvest and blessings. Whatever any of them had sown, they were about to see the payoff.

By not allowing Rachel to come into a place of abundance "in sin," God was really bestowing mercy on her. We, as believers, need to understand this also. If we are doing what is right in the eyes of the Lord, there is no reason for us to be full of sorrow. As God told Cain in Genesis 4:7, "If you do well, will you not be accepted? And if you do not do well, sin lies at the door. And its desire is for you, but you should rule over it." We also read a new testament scripture that points to this as well. In Romans 6:19-21:

> I speak in human terms because of the weakness of your flesh. For just as you presented your members as slaves of uncleanness, and of lawlessness leading to more lawlessness, so now present your members as slaves of righteousness for holiness. For when you were slaves of sin, you were free in regard to righteousness. What fruit did you have then in the things of which you are now ashamed? For the end of those things is death.

Kim: The key thing is that human nature hasn't really changed. We see the same human nature now as we read

about regarding the 17th century in our history books. This
is just what went on, and we are all linked one with another
based on our humanity. So what hurts and frustrates someone
today is the same thing that could have just as easily hurt and
frustrated the men and women of yesterday.

Pastor B: A final point we want to make about Rachel is that she
purposes to ask her sister Leah for the mandrakes she sees her
nephew, Reuben, bring in from the field. In understanding
the purpose of mandrakes, we know they are said to be made
of a narcotic substance and considered a herb that would help
stimulate fertility. This brings to mind a couple of thoughts
that address some popular behaviors of single, Christian
females of today. It is very popular for young ladies to go to
specialty stores that sell these absolutely scanty, sexy, skimpy
underwear and spend tons of money on this stuff. They say
they are walking in an abstinent lifestyle, yet, they frustrate
themselves by wearing these undergarments, and no one is to
see this underwear on them but their mothers, right?

I remember when I was in my twenties and thought
I was "all that." I was not buying my undergarments just
so I could look at me in the mirror. I mean, I would look at
me in the mirror and after I was so, so very pleased with
what was staring back at me, then I certainly wanted some
brother to see, too. I even had a girlfriend who would buy
the most gorgeous underwear Pogues (a department store
that used to be in Cincinnati) had to offer. She would strut
and dance around her apartment, with her very tiny self, in
her underwear and a fashion chain around her waist, draping
down over her belly-button, as she listened to Marvin Gaye
and Al Green sing to her from her stereo. A few telephone
calls later and the next thing we knew she had plans for
the night . . . all night! She too, like me, was a very carnal
Christian at the time, but thanks be to God, she turned her
life around while she was still young and today serves God

out of a truly faithful and sweet, sweet spirit.

Another thing many young, single women do is go to the specialty stores and purchase these scented candles by the dozens. We have enough flames going in some of these apartments, bedrooms, and homes to heat Alaska! We have put on our sexy underwear, lit our candles, slathered in our oils and fragrances, not to mention popped in our favorite "mood" music or video and if any single woman can have a steady diet of that and not feel sexually tempted, I say more power to her! That sister is superbad all by herself! For me, this sounds like the biggest aphrodisiac going. The Bible clearly says, and says it imperatively, "FLEE FORNICATION!" If there are no plans to fornicate or commit adultery after all of this preparation, and one becomes stimulated, the only out they have is to masturbate.

This is the same as Rachel's desire for those narcotic laden mandrakes. Those mandrakes would have had her in a most excited, sexy, sassy mood, and that was fine because she was married. While the specialty shops that sell the undies, oils, perfumes and candles are not selling mandrakes, those items can still have the same intoxicating affect. So what are your thoughts about the oils, candles, undies, music and this stimulating atmosphere, Kim?

Kim: We know, according to scripture, that the idea of the oil and incense was a very important part of the atmosphere God wanted set in the Tabernacle. God commanded the children of Israel to make certain fragrances just for the tabernacle, but not to ever make those fragrances for themselves. He said it was for Him and Him alone. He would not have told them not to do this if He didn't already know in His foreknowledge that they would have wanted those fragrances for their personal use. God wanted those fragrances to set an atmosphere of worship and sacrifice unto Him. When single people get into this, and they know it will result in sinful behavior, then it is the same as Aaron's sons coming to the Holy place and offering up strange fire unto the Lord. We have sexual fires that burn in us and the Bible says in 1Peter 2:9:

> *But you are a chosen generation, a royal priesthood, a holy nation, His own special people, that you may proclaim the praises of Him who called you out of darkness into His marvelous light;*

We cannot afford to set these fires and have no way to put them out. If we sow the seeds of these wrong behaviors, the end result is guilt and condemnation.

Pastor B: This is why we have the end result of tears and pain over and over again. The only thing left for these frustrated persons is to come dragging into church with all their depression and despair as they wait on the pastor to preach them happy, and the choir to sing them into oblivion. They want somebody to please pray for them so that their pain will pass. It is high time the church become more triumphant with people coming to church with an expectation for God to move mightily as He desires, as opposed to the need to keep working through these same issues with the same people over and over again. I would like to say, however, that I believe the mature Christian can light candles, have fragrances, and use that as a setting to invoke the presence of the Lord. The Bible says in 1 Corinthians 7 that the single person cares for the things of the Lord and how to please Him. I believe if someone more mature can produce that kind of atmosphere, without becoming tempted toward wrong behaviors, it would be beautiful indeed. That would be wonderful for an atmosphere in which to worship the Lord.

Kim, we will just watch the Lord and see how He begins to bring the church to the table so as to prepare us to be more candid about these issues in the days ahead. I want to thank you so much for assisting me and sharing your research, and taking time to have this talk with me about the subject of masturbation. It has been wonderful. Thank you very much.

Kim: You're welcome. Thank you.

Post Dialogue

PERHAPS IT MAY SEEM that the dialogue made too much of the issue of masturbation. I do not think too much can be said about it at this time in the life of the Church. It is truly one of the biggest secret sins in the Church. It is with total confidence in who He was, as the Son of God, with no fear of retribution, that our Savior could say to His disciples in John 14:30:

> *I will no longer talk much with you, for the ruler of this world is coming, and he has nothing in Me.*

We must choose to get serious with God over these issues. God will honor the heart that is willing to "fess-up" to a weakness in this area. The biggest problem we have with God is not so much the doing of the sin, whatever it is, but the bigger infraction is of not confessing to Him anything about it! The bottom line is the fact that we had already committed the sin in our heart before we physically carried it out. His disappointment is when we call ourselves hiding it from Him. It is like the prophet, Nathan, having to come and tell David about the sin David committed with Bathsheba. Why was David, who was most assuredly a prophetic man, so far removed from the message Nathan gave him? As Nathan was yet speaking, David should have known this message from Nathan was pointing toward the sexual sin and murder he committed. As a matter of fact, when he saw Nathan coming toward him he should have guessed this was going to be a "bad hair day" . . . he should have known what was coming. If we confess our sexually inappropriate behaviors to the Lord, we will begin to "de-seed" ourselves of the enemy's seed in us! Bringing dark issues to the marvelous light of Christ is how we kill off this harmful spiritual disease that needs dark, damp places in which to breed.

Rachel Revisited

Whenever we are full of sorrow, it is because we are not walking in the place God would have us to walk on a consistent basis. Usually a little heart inspection will reveal the source of the problem. If we then pray it through with the Lord and make our necessary adjustments, God will quickly heal and deliver us from sorrow and sadness of heart. A final key point I would like to bring out is that this city Ephrath, or Ephrathah, is also the same city that was later renamed Bethlehem. The Lord was not going to allow Rachel to set foot in the same city that would become the birthplace of the Savior of this world, when He knew full well that Rachel had this problem with idolatry. This is based solely on a spiritual law and the prophetic move of God that would later unfold. I will clarify this in a moment. The Bible says that whatever territory our feet walk upon, we possess (Joshua 1:3). Due to this spiritual law being at work, if Rachel even set foot on that territory it would taint the spiritual destiny of Jesus being born there, so her continuing to live, unfortunately, just could not be.

Now let's look at Genesis 35:22c – 26:

Now the sons of Jacob were twelve: the sons of Leah were Reuben, Jacob's firstborn, and Simeon, Levi, Judah, Issachar, and Zebulun; the sons of Rachel were Joseph and Benjamin; the sons of Bilhah, Rachel's maidservant, were Dan and Naphtali; and the sons of Zilpah, Leah's maidservant, were Gad and Asher. These were the sons of Jacob who were born to him in Padan Aram.

In verse 23 we clearly see that Judah is the son of Jacob, born to Leah. In the following verse 24, we see that his son Joseph, also born to Jacob, was through his wife Rachel. Now both of these women were extremely important in the prophetic events that would be preparatory to Jesus' birth. One woman was an ancestral grandmother, the other an ancestral aunt. Jesus is Our Lord, He is Our Savior, but He is also known as the Lion of the tribe of Judah. In the 49th chapter of Genesis, as Jacob (Israel) prepares to die, he assembles his sons together, as is Jewish custom, to bless them. Let us take a look at the prophetic blessings spoken over Leah's son, Judah and Rachel's son, Joseph. Genesis 49:8 – 12 and 22 – 26:

> *Judah, you are he whom your brothers shall praise; Your hand shall be on the neck of your enemies; Your father's children shall bow down before you. Judah is a lion's whelp; From the prey, my son, you have gone up. He bows down, he lies down as a lion; And as a lion, who shall rouse him? The scepter shall not depart from Judah, Nor a lawgiver from between his feet, Until Shiloh comes; And to Him shall be the obedience of the people. Binding his donkey to the vine, And his donkey's colt to the choice vine, He washed his garments in wine, And his clothes in the blood of grapes. His eyes are darker than wine, And his teeth whiter than milk.*

> *"Joseph is a fruitful bough, A fruitful bough by a well; His branches run over the wall. The archers have bitterly grieved him, Shot at him and hated him. But his bow remained in strength, And the arms of his hands were made strong By the hands of the Mighty God of Jacob (From there is the Shepherd, the Stone of Israel), By the God of your father who will help you, And by the Almighty who will bless you With blessings of heaven above, Blessings of the deep that lies beneath, Blessings of the breasts and of the womb. The blessings of your father Have excelled the blessings of my ancestors, Up to the utmost bound of the everlasting hills. They shall be on the head of Joseph, And on the crown of the head of him who was separate from his brothers.*

What God ended up doing was have these women work in conjunction with one another. As much as they were at odds with one another, they had no idea they were spiritual partners to get Jesus to the earth! The Word of God to Judah was speaking about Our Savior who was to come, so Leah was responsible for that part of the plan of God . . . extremely major! However, without the greatest strategic planning on God's part, Judah would have perished! BUT GOD! It was Rachel who birthed Joseph. Joseph was the one instrumental in bringing the twelve tribes of Israel into one land and saving all of them from the famine that had come to Canaan! The twelve tribes settled in Goshen and were there for 430 years as one people, until God delivered them from slavery through His servant Moses. Rachel was not as fruitful as she desired to be, but it was she who birthed the son that was referred to as " . . . a fruitful bough . . . " Look at the millions that were delivered by the strong and mighty hand of God. Just look at Cecil B. DeMille's movie, *The Ten Commandments* (smile)! This happened because Joseph chose to obey God from his youth. Even though his mother died, God let the soles of Joseph's feet touch down in Ephrath and the blessing of the "fruitfulness" of that land was his! Isn't God wonderful?! He will always make fruitful those who are obedient to His Word.

The only thing any of us have to do is what Spike Lee says (even though he wasn't the first one to say it): "DO THE RIGHT THING!" We cannot have God, and then have our "little stuff," our little idol gods, our little sexual sins, over on the side like some side salad to the main course! The Lord is the main course and He is not interested in having any other food on the table with Him!

How very sad for Rachel that she personally did not experience the fruitfulness of God. What is more so, how very sad for any person today trapped in some sick behavior and cannot seem to find a way out. There are thousands of persons attempting to serve God on one hand, but yielding to the works of the enemy on the other.

A Changed Mind Brings Fresh Revelation

PAUL WAS GREATLY DISTURBED by the church in Corinth and said so in his second letter to them. We read in 2 Corinthians 12:21:

> *... lest, when I come again, my God will humble me among you, and I shall mourn for many who have sinned before and have not repented of the uncleanness, fornication, and lewdness which they have practiced.*

Paul saw himself doing nothing short of weeping and repenting on their behalf, right in their presence. He knew they had not repented of these things themselves. He knew it would be a sovereign move of God to have him do this and it would be quite humbling, to say the least. This was by no means an issue to be viewed or taken lightly, as many of us have done in the church today. We cannot allow ourselves to be the breeding ground for satan. Some of us truly want God at a deeper level; this is truly our heart's cry. We can say like Paul said in Philippians 3:12-14, as we begin to confess these weaknesses:

> *Not that I have already attained, or am already perfected; but I press on, that I may lay hold of that for which Christ Jesus has also laid hold of me. Brethren, I do not count myself to have apprehended; but one thing I do, forgetting those things which are behind and reaching forward to those things which are ahead, I press toward the goal for the prize of the upward call of God in Christ Jesus.*

As Paul lived out this celibate lifestyle and his commitment to God, I believe it was not unlike Moses who stayed apart from his wife for forty days and nights, so that he could seek the face of God; in which he received the revelation of the commandments of God written in stone. I believe Paul is not unlike Anna and Simeon who were the precious ones summoned by the Spirit of God to come to the circumcision of Jesus Christ, and to behold with their own eyes the revelation all Israel had been awaiting. I believe Paul is not unlike John the Baptist who both saw and spoke the revelation that Jesus Christ was the Lamb of God that had come to take away the sin of the world. I believe that God showed and revealed to Paul things that others could not see or understand. This is why Paul was the one selected by God to write two-thirds of the New Testament. He was also the one that had the awesome experience we read of in 2 Corinthians 12:1-4:

> It is doubtless not profitable for me to boast. I will come to visions and revelations of the Lord: I know a man in Christ who fourteen years ago--whether in the body I do not know, or whether out of the body I do not know, God knows--such a one was caught up to the third heaven. And I know such a man--whether in the body or out of the body I do not know, God knows-- how he was caught up into Paradise and heard inexpressible words, which it is not lawful for a man to utter.

Saints, we are believing God for a greater outpouring of His Spirit. The prerequisites for this is the cleansing of our own temples along with fasting and prayer. This brings to mind something I experienced at an evening service in the Caribbean. I was led by the Lord to wear a particular dress that evening. The dress was to the knee, low neckline (no cleavage exposed; as a matter of fact I couldn't make cleavage if I tried, smile), low back (right above the backbone/shoulder area), and was fitted at the waist. I really did not feel and sense the cold and judgmental spirit that was closing in on me until I was in the church service. Some people thought I made a bad choice in clothing. The Lord spoke to my heart and said, "Many think you have defiled My Temple by your attire, but I am concerned about people's hearts more than people's clothes. If My people would take as much care fixing up the inside of their temple (self) as they do fixing up the outside of it, I would be more glorified in the earth!" This brought to mind a prophetic word of God spoken by the Old Testament prophet Haggai. In chapter two verse nine it says:

> *The glory of this latter temple shall be greater than the former,' says the LORD of hosts. 'And in this place I will give peace,' says the LORD of hosts.*

After service was over there were two sweethearts who came up to me, who are not only sisters in the Lord, but are biological sisters to one another, as well. The unconditional love they showed to me is what helped me get through the remainder of the evening. Upon arrival back to my hotel room that evening, the Lord had to truly help me out in prayer. He said to me, "the nakedness of well covered up, beautifully appareled, religious, immoral bodies does not glorify me." He said, "they are NOT COVERED in garments of worship, they are NOT CLOAKED and COVERED in humility, NOT COVERED and VESTED in my love . . . just well covered up, naked, smelly bodies that pretend!" He said, "if their stares and attitudes made you feel cold, how do you think it feels to Me? It breaks My heart."

On the next morning at the church, the Lord finally ministered to me. A question was asked of the prophetic team on another issue, and I grabbed the response and allowed it to minister to my spirit and soul which was still reeling from my emotions over the previous evening's service. The man of God that was ministering that morning said during the question and answer session, "You have to be free of the fear of being criticized."

I am certainly of the persuasion that one should stand strong about those things which one feels passionately. *The idea of dealing with sexual sin in the church, addressing it and no longer sweeping it under the rug* is truly a passion of mine on which I take a very strong stand. I am of the mind that a great many ills of the church, with regard to our weaknesses over all manner of sexual impropriety, be it masturbation, fornication, adultery, the love of pornography, etc., could be healed if we would just get honest with ourselves and the Lord, and deal with these skeletons in our closets. I feel that pastoral counseling, confessing the sins, support groups, deliverance ministry, as well as fasting and prayer are tools God has given us to aid in our becoming healed and whole in this area of our life.

Maximize the Spirit, Minimize the Flesh

Again, we know that Adam and Eve were experiencing a wonderfully, spiritual relationship with their Heavenly Father before they sinned. The life they lived before they fell is summed up in Galatians 5:16–18:

> *I say then: Walk in the Spirit, and you shall not fulfill the lust of the flesh. For the flesh lusts against the Spirit, and the Spirit against the flesh; and these are contrary to one another, so that you do not do the things that you wish. But if you are led by the Spirit, you are not under the law.*

The only life we Christians are to be living is a life in the Spirit. This life in the spirit was not printed in the Bible as something to be considered lightly by us Christians. We need to truly understand that the enemy will have his guns loaded against the church if thousands of Christians were to suddenly repent and begin to walk in a holy lifestyle. When these lifestyle changes begin to occur, the success for each and every individual will be predicated upon whether or not we were willing to do this by the spirit, or try this thing in the flesh. If by the flesh you think you will accomplish your much needed deliverance, stopping the sexual sin, walking in holiness, you are already earmarked for failure. One of the things I believe will begin to happen, if this is dealt with by the flesh, is we will see even greater manifestations of the works of the flesh. As we further read in Galatians 5:19–21:

Now the works of the flesh are evident, which are: adultery, fornication, uncleanness, lewdness, idolatry, sorcery, hatred, contentions, jealousies, outbursts of wrath, selfish ambitions, dissensions, heresies, envy, murders, drunkenness, revelries, and the like; of which I tell you beforehand, just as I also told you in time past, that those who practice such things will not inherit the kingdom of God.

I believe we will even begin to see a greater flood of this perverse behavior erupt in the church unless we follow the guidelines the Lord has laid out for each of us. Don't you find it amazing that in the Galatians 5:19–21 list of sins, the first four on the list reflect sexually immoral behaviors, and the next two on the list have to do with idolatry? Just stop and think about this? When I was a little girl, this mega-church theory was unheard of. If a church had anywhere from 100 to 200 members, they were considered very successful. Well, here we are with churches bursting at the seams with 2000 to 5000 members and some 10,000 members, and the sexual sin in the church is getting worse and worse all the time, not better. Why? I believe it is because people are trying to walk this out in the flesh. From the late 70's until the mid 80's the church had the greatest knowledge explosion it had ever known. We learned more about the things of God than any other church age known to man. Now there are those that would argue and say that it is all relative, I say NO. The percentage of sexual sin in the mega churches is not relative to the percentages that existed in the smaller churches of the 50's and 60's. The more WORD of GOD we learned, the more the enemy intended to make a mockery out of the church, and unfortunately, we have allowed him to do just that.

When Adam and Eve fell through sin, they lost their original estate with God (which was spiritual) and sexual sin has been on the rise ever since. We clearly see there is certainly more revelation knowledge about God today than there was yesterday. If more knowledge of God and more people in churches was the key, why are we having these problems at epidemic proportions? It's because sin continues to wax bolder and bolder! The enemy does not care how much WORD we know, he looks at how much WORD we do!

Incubus And Succubus

THIS CHAPTER WILL LOOK at another area of concern, those things that can happen to us while we sleep. Praise be to God that the spirit-man in the Christian never sleeps. If he did, we Christians would really become fair game for the enemy.

Some Christians may have never heard these words in the chapter title, Incubus and Succubus, but it is now time we all become aware of these words in that they are the names of sexual demonic forces. The first word, incubus, is pronounced "in – key – bus." The second word, succubus, is pronounced "suck – ee – bus."

So as to help you the reader, it would be good to start with authenticating these words. So, let's start by looking at the definitions of these words as they are listed in *Merriam-Webster's Collegiate Dictionary, 10th ed., s.v.:*

> *incubus: an evil spirit that lies on persons in their sleep; esp: one that has sexual intercourse with women while they are sleeping*

> *succubus: a demon assuming female form to have sexual intercourse with men in their sleep.*

Sexual desire is one of the most powerful drives in human beings; therefore, satan is constantly exploiting this area in the lives of people. Without a doubt, this issue of demonic forces sexually victimizing persons of all ages creates some serious problems for Christians who are ignorant of the truth. Now, like anything else, there is the camp of unfortunate souls who readily welcome the visitations of these evil spirits because of the mind-blowing pleasures these spirits bring as a means of seducing these persons. For those persons who have had this horrendous experience and would choose to never have those kinds of encounters again, it would first take a made-up mind on the part of the person to have nothing ever again to do with these spiritual forces. Secondly, it may mean the added benefit of fasting and prayer so as to stand in real victory in this area.

It is not by accident I have allowed this chapter to follow the dialogue on masturbation. It is certainly a well orchestrated plan of the enemy to go after those persons who routinely engage in and experiment with sexual sin. That is just the nature of the beast. These spirits will also attempt to prey upon any person in Christian leadership. Especially if the leader has potential in the realm of true spiritual power and anointing, as well as having influence enough to advance the purposes of the Kingdom of God.

Now, as the definitions state, these spirits victimize sleeping persons. Well, that is not always the case. These spirits are known to also visit persons when they are in a somewhat twilight sleep or when wide awake. I have talked with several persons who have had this experience and each person was rather unclear as to what was actually happening because it seemed so much like a dream/nightmare. They replayed the event over and over in their mind trying to make sure they were not hallucinating. The sexual sensations were real. They could sense a true presence of something not human, and at the time the spiritual beings were in the room with them they were always inundated with a sense of powerlessness or helplessness. What the common theme is, however, is that many times they catch the person off guard. It is amazing to me the number of persons I have talked with who have had this experience right after a major breakthrough to a new spiritual level in their walk with the Lord. One woman had this experience immediately after a tremendous time of worship in the presence of the Lord. She had just fallen asleep and was then awakened. A second woman had a visitation after having been ordained and was awakened in the wee hours of early morning as she was lying comfortably next to her sleeping husband. Lastly, a third woman had the experience while away on vacation with other Christian women after they had sat up laughing and talking late one night. In these particular cases, the women state sex was not on their minds at all when these visitations occurred.

The danger in toying with these spirits, even for a moment, is not knowing when this whole situation will turn progressively destructive. It eventually is going to get out of hand, because the devil comes only to steal, kill, and destroy. Since that is his mission on earth, everything he does ultimately results in fulfilling his purposes and his purposes alone. These spirits are doing nothing more than raping those persons that allow them liberality in their life. Yes, these demonic forces bring immense pleasure at first, but how soon one forgets that payday is coming! These spirits are not going to allow anyone to experience only pleasure without trying to hurt them as well. Another strategy these spirits have in some cases is bringing a person to the point of almost experiencing orgasm, but then abruptly stopping short of it, just so the person will have to engage in masturbating. This is what they want the persons to do anyway, because the enemy knows these actions are displeasing to the Lord.

The now deceased Win Worley best summarized the end result of what these demonic forces do to anyone who would engage them in these God-forsaken activities. Worley, who was a noted expert on the subject of demon powers and activity, in his book, "Conquering The Hosts of Hell," wrote:

> "These depraved spirits play with their captives, cruelly tormenting and using their bodies to satisfy the orgiastic and filthy cravings of the demons. Once entrenched, they do not care whether or not the experience is pleasant for their host. As a matter of fact, they rather prefer that it produce pain and suffering. This way they not only enjoy the lust they generate but also the horror with which the cringing and hapless person is filled as, again and again, he is driven to do what he has come to hate and dread. The lower the person can be made to sink, the

*more animalistic and sickeningly filthy he becomes, the more the
demons enjoy their cruel game."*

    We Christians must always remind ourselves of the fact that
we are spirit; we have a soul and live in a body. The emphasis must
always be placed on the fact that we are spiritual beings first and
foremost. Paul, in writing to the church in Thessalonica stated that
he desired the saints' spirit, soul and body, in being sanctified by God,
be maintained in preserved blamelessness (1 Thessalonians 5:23).
    The point I want to make is that God is Spirit, and we are
made in His likeness and image, therefore we are spirit. It stands to
reason that the enemy, who is also spirit, will most assuredly go after
God's spiritual children. Many people have relegated this information
about the incubi and succubi to mere folklore and tales. We do
ourselves a grave injustice if we continue with such assumptions. On
the one hand, man constantly says validation only comes with the
proving; but on the other hand, he knows there are many areas that
yet remain darkened and hidden to his understanding. God refuses
to be reduced to the abject reasoning and conclusions of man. In the
Old Testament the Bible speaks of the fall from heaven of Lucifer and
a third of the angels. Now I ask you, where in the world do we think
they are and what do we think they are doing? Do we think they
are just twiddling their thumbs until Jesus Christ returns to get His
church? Do we think they decided to be ever so sweet and kind since
they already blew it in heaven, and they don't want to make God
angry while they are in the earth by bothering His people? Wake up,
Wake up, Wake up!! We are in the midst of the most powerful war
ever! It is a wicked and evil war plotted by the enemy in which he
has marshaled all of his forces to strategically go after the children of
God. Why? Because he hates us and will get rid of us by any means
necessary . . . whatever it takes! Praise God for those of us who are
aware of the realm of the spirit and the weaponry we have already
been given by our God to deal with the works of darkness!
    Those of you who would like to read more information
on Incubus and Succubus need only make a visit to your local
neighborhood library. Most libraries have information in the

reference section. You may be very surprised by the information you find.

The Crucifixion And Circumcision

I AM SO GLAD the event of the Crucifixion happened long ago and not during my lifetime. After all, with the technology we have today, had Jesus' death at Calvary happened in our lifetime there would have been lights and cameras filming the entire gory scene, along with your on-the-spot-roving reporter's blow-by-blow account of it all. God forbid!

In recent years (the past twenty plus) we have learned that the crucifixion process was truly beyond human comprehension. Even though crucifixion was the corporal punishment of the day used by the Roman government, still Jesus' crucifixion was the worst ever, and at the same time, the holiest!

In the previous chapters I have attempted to point out some similarities between the first Adam and the second Adam, Jesus Christ. The whole notion of "the tree of knowledge of good and evil," as the tree Adam and Eve touched, being the result of their engaging in sex, is difficult to understand unless we remember there was something of which God did not want them to have knowledge. Something He did not want them to know. Just as Lucifer, now satan, discovered the iniquity in himself, he also uncovered the source of the iniquity in Adam. The tendency toward the iniquity was always there because God created both the angels and mankind as free moral agents, not as controlled robots with His superimposed will upon them. He was and still is a God of choice.

As I write this last chapter of the book, a bittersweet moment seems to creep upon me. I feel as if I am leaving a very good friend, and am coming to the concluding moments of our time spent together. It was with many tears that I wrote this concluding chapter, because the revelation from Our Father was just that precious and yet earth-shakingly powerful. Again, I will solicit you to remain as free and open in your thinking as possible. There is a fictional passage I have couched within the contents of this chapter so it will help clarify the scriptural truths that are being shared. Think of it as a parable.

God never wanted Adam and Eve to know the power of destruction the uncovering of iniquity would bring. Well, in Lucifer's case, God just kicked him out of heaven and was done with him as the covering cherub, and he then became satan. However, God was not going to give up on mankind even though He had to kick them out of the Garden. Praise God! So the only way God could right the wrong was to cause the shedding of blood. Why blood? Because all "life" is in the blood. The prophet Ezekiel says in Ezekiel 16:6:

> And when I passed by you and saw you struggling in your own blood, I said to you in your blood, 'Live!' Yes, I said to you in your blood, 'Live!'

When satan tricked man with his "deathblow," man's eternal fate was sealed with a spiritual death. God, therefore, had to counter this fatality with life. God proceeded with slaying animals, shedding their blood so as to cover Adam and Eve's sin, and then made tunics of skin to clothe them (Genesis 3:21). If bloodshed was all that was important, God could have just slain the animals and allowed Adam and Eve to remain naked. God, however, could no longer look upon this defiled tree, Adam's penis, or Eve's garden (no longer enclosed), her vagina because they were now unclean. Their nakedness was once pure before both themselves and Him, but the stain of sin had now birthed shame in His created beings. So He was covering them for their sakes. The scripture says in Hebrews 4:13:

> And there is no creature hidden from His sight, but all things are naked and open to the eyes of Him to whom we must give account.

Fortunately for us, God's mercy allows us to benefit from

Him covering up any of those areas in our lives that cause us shame. He does so with His own type of "spiritual animal skins," until we come of spiritual age and maturity, at which time we are finally able to confront those issues head on. The "spiritual animal skins" God uses to cover us are His unending mercy, His sometimes private restoration of us without letting "our secret" out, His tender and loving nudgings in the still of the night on the quiet of our pillow. He is even gracious and loving enough as to allow some of His children to remain covered for the entirety of their Christian walk because they never come to maturity in the Lord. How unfortunate for His people and how unfortunate a loss for the Body of Christ.

The Bible clearly says man is like a tree and that the tree would bring forth its fruit in its season. We know purely on a physiological level that when a man's penis is erect and ejaculates semen into the vaginal area of a woman, he releases into her the potential for pregnancy, if there is an egg available to be fertilized. The man's sperm is his fruitfulness and the woman's eggs are her fruitfulness. Earlier in the book I shared what could have been God's prototype for birth. Either man or woman would pull beings out of themselves as God pulled Eve out of Adam; or there would be a conversation, by the spirit of agreement, between a husband and wife as God had with the Virgin Mary when Jesus was conceived, which would result in a newborn baby. What is of interest here, however, is the bloodshed required on the parts of both male and female. For the female it is once a month, every month during her childbearing years and for the male it is a once in a lifetime event, which God called circumcision. Now you are probably asking what does the crucifixion have to do with circumcision? Well, in a direct sense it is not apparent, but indirectly there was a purpose that eventually would be linked to Jesus Christ.

When God commanded Adam and Eve not to so much as touch the tree, and they touched it anyway, that was the first stage of the ultimate fall. When the touch happened, Adam's body was defiled. We know from a spiritual standpoint that nothing defiled can come into the presence of God. What did God eventually do? He established a covenant relationship with Abraham many years later, not unlike what He once shared with Adam.

From Adam until Abraham God looked upon the bloodshed and sacrifices of animals as sufficient. Who could possibly account for the longing that was in God's heart—to be close to His "little ones" again? Finally the blood of animals was not enough, so approximately 2000 years later He forms this beautiful relationship with His son Abraham, who was then called Abram. God begins to test and try Abram on many different levels and God always found Abram operating in "God-like" faith. They had many close encounters of the most wonderful kind. This pleased God so much, that God came to Abram and began to reveal to Abram His plan for their covenant relationship. First of all Abram's name was changed to Abraham, Genesis 17:5. Secondly, God spoke to him of a physiological change God wanted made in Abraham's body so as to ratify the covenant. In Genesis 17:10-13 we read:

> *This is My covenant which you shall keep, between Me and you and your descendants after you: Every male child among you shall be circumcised; and you shall be circumcised in the flesh of your foreskins, and it shall be a sign of the covenant between Me and you. He who is eight days old among you shall be circumcised, every male child in your generations, he who is born in your house or bought with money from any foreigner who is not your descendant. He who is born in your house and he who is bought with your money must be circumcised, and My covenant shall be in your flesh for an everlasting covenant.*

In the words of my spiritual father, "God told Abraham, son I'm going to hit you where it hurts!" This was God's way of making sure the tree could be made sanctified. The Bible says in Leviticus 17:11:

> *"For the life of the flesh is in the blood, and I have given it to you upon the altar to make atonement for your souls; for it is the blood that makes atonement for the soul."*

We know there is no remission of sin without the shedding of blood (Hebrews 9:22), and the scripture says by bloodshed almost all things are purged. We see that it was necessary for God to cause blood to be shed from the "body parts" that were members used in the act of unrighteousness. For man he makes this a one time event, but for women it is a monthly event, because each time sperm meets with an egg there is the potential for life. Even when the wedding night occurs and the hymen tissue is broken, man has access to that which will bring him pleasures untold, but it is certainly not without bloodshed first on the part of the wife.

Now let's move up to the time of the birth and life of Jesus Christ. Another 2000 years have passed and God has now made provision to come into the home stretch with His plan. From the beginning, Jesus came into the ministry knowing His Father's will for His life on this earth. He knew He came to die, to die for us all. Jesus knew all too well the prophetic words that had been declared about Him for centuries, and He knew the Psalms. He couldn't possibly be prepared in His mind ahead of time, however, for the travesty His physical body would ultimately have to suffer. We human beings, in our finite thinking, know that our minds cannot really conceptualize pain until we are in it. Jesus prayed in the famous Garden of Gethsemene Prayer that His Father would allow the bitter cup of death to pass . . . He prayed not once, but three times. He received a glimpse from the Father, of what really lay ahead. He wanted so much for there to be another way, but in the full scheme of things, as it pertained to redemption, there was but one plan, the one laid out before the foundation of the world. Again remember, God is a God of choice, and Jesus had the option of backing out of what was facing Him altogether, and if Jesus desired, on top of it, God would send angels to deliver Him (Matthew 26:53). Jesus made up His mind long, long before that day came that He would always obey the will of His Father, no matter the price to pay. Jesus made His decision to carry on, and His loving Father still sent reinforcement in the person of an angel who came and strengthened Him in those final hours (Luke 22:43).

Most of us know the story of the "Crucifixion." There are different accounts, based on the disciple's different experiences of the events as they witnessed them. I will focus on the account in Matthew and John because they give some critical details, which serve to emphasize what was happening in the earth as Christ was dying. We read in Matthew 27:45-53:

> *Now from the sixth hour until the ninth hour there was darkness over all the land. And about the ninth hour Jesus cried out with a loud voice, saying, "Eli, Eli, lama sabachthani?" that is, "My God, My God, why have You forsaken Me?" Some of those who stood there, when they heard that, said, "This Man is calling for Elijah!" Immediately one of them ran and took a sponge, filled it with sour wine and put it on a reed, and offered it to Him to drink. The rest said, "Let Him alone; let us see if Elijah will come to save Him." And Jesus cried out again with a loud voice, and yielded up His spirit. Then, behold, the veil of the temple was torn in two from top to bottom; and the earth quaked, and the rocks were split, and the graves were opened; and many bodies of the saints who had fallen asleep were raised; and coming out of the graves after His resurrection, they went into the holy city and appeared to many.*

We also read in John 19:25-30:

> *Now there stood by the cross of Jesus His mother, and His mother's sister, Mary the wife of Clopas, and Mary Magdalene. When Jesus therefore saw His mother, and the disciple whom He loved standing by, He said to His mother, "Woman, behold your son!" Then He said to the disciple, "Behold your mother!" And from that hour that disciple took her to his own home.*
>
> *After this, Jesus, knowing that all things were now accomplished, that the Scripture might be fulfilled, said, "I thirst!" Now a vessel full of sour wine was sitting there; and they filled a sponge with sour wine, put it on hyssop, and put it to His mouth. So when Jesus had received the sour wine, He said, "It is finished!" And bowing His head, He gave up His spirit.*

There has never been nor will there ever be anyone known to man who will have endured what Jesus had to suffer in dying on the cross for an entire lost and sinful world. The agony of His death was not merely the crucifixion process, the agony was the spiritual death. The bearing of untold millions of lives because of the sin nature that was in the universe! That was the agony . . . the taking away of the sin of the world! This is the travesty He glimpsed in the Garden as His sweat was as great drops of blood! (Luke 22:44)

Jesus was triumphant until the very end. Remember, He was winning back mankind's right standing with God, and also establishing the victorious and triumphant church. Jesus Christ is the dying Savior, but He's also the dying Bridegroom. He is dying for the church, His beautiful Bride and He loves Her madly!

WOMEN, TELL ME, how many of you like a weak, whining wimp of a man? How many of you find that type of man appealing? No woman likes that kind of man, even those who mistakenly think they want to control a man, or control their husbands. If he were to allow her to do so, that same woman would then want to turn him around and kick him square in his "seat of decision" for giving in to her! There was never a point in time when Jesus acted like or talked like He was weak-willed, faltering, and losing sight of God's purpose and vision for the wife of His choice, the Church! NEVER!

I had the tremendous privilege in 1977 of sitting under the teaching of a very anointed and dynamic teacher of the Word. She taught that the Jesus Christ we read about in scripture was triumphant and conquering when He cried out in agony on the cross! He wasn't whining and pining with a "Oh, woe is me" attitude. Even in this most cruel and grueling physical pain, He was declaring a strong victory as He crossed the finish line! I learned that the following passage of scripture seems to be more accurately translated in a particular version she shared with us while teaching. His cry of, "Eli, Eli, lama sabachthani?" was not "My God, My God, why hast thou forsaken me?" This was the mighty Son of the Living God! This was the One who withstood satan for forty days and forty nights in the wilderness as He beheld all the kingdoms of this world in a moment of time. This was the One that was tempted with every temptation known to man and never, ever yielded to even a split-second of sin. This was the One that walked on the water, opened blinded eyes, healed the sick, raised the dead, peered into the hearts of men and spoke to the hidden iniquity housed therein and now all of a sudden He's going limp and weak? NO! NO! NO! What He said on the cross was, "My God! My God! For this cause I was spared!" ("spared" meaning given or sent on assignment). In other words this is the reason I have been sent here on assignment. This teaching with regard to this particular scripture is printed in *The Lamsa Translation of the Bible*, by George Lamsa. Jesus was fulfilling "purpose" up until the absolute last minutes of his life, and doing it victoriously! I believe this is the only conclusion that makes any scriptural sense. Why would His cry capture the attention of anyone's ears unless it was loud and with authority? Why would His cry capture their attention if it was the usual whining that all those who had gone the way of crucifixion were known to do? It captured their attention because it was an exclamation of triumph, NOT DEFEAT!

This flows perfectly with the account of Him in Psalms 22:24 and His revelatory prayer in John 16:32:

> For He has not despised nor abhorred the affliction of the afflicted; Nor has He hidden His face from Him; but when He cried to Him, He heard.

> Indeed the hour is coming, yes, has now come, that you will be scattered, each to his own, and will leave Me alone. And yet I am not alone, because the Father is with Me.

God did not turn away from His only begotten Son. He was right there from the beginning through the entire horrible mess! It was horrible, despicable, but HOLY! Why would the God we serve promise us mere mortals, in Hebrews 13:5b, who are laden with so much sin, " . . . I will never leave you nor forsake you"? As dirty and filthy as we are, as wicked, (2 Chronicles 7:14) and sinful, (Romans

3:23), as we are, He is not going to pull out on us, but pull out on Jesus? Psalm 139 tells us that even if we make our bed in hell, He will be there! Yet we believe the Great Omniscient, Omnipresent, Omnipotent God is bailing out on the only Son He has, who has been nothing less than faithful and true for His entire 33 ½ years of living in a totally corrupt, sinful world, at the greatest hour of agony He has ever known! Are we crazy to really believe this? All of a sudden, as the young people say, "He's going to step, God is going to step!" Saints, just stop and think for a moment of all the times God not only delivered you from one royal mess after another (that you got yourself into, mind you), but to add insult to injury, He was there and His ministering angels were there as well. Think about where we have dragged Him to in the name of "doing our thing," and when the tears come, as they always do, He is Johnny-on-the-spot to forgive us and reassure us He will put it under His blood. God is far too good and merciful to do such a thing as being there for us but not His Son! We need to get this revelation, get it right and get it now! There is absolutely nothing we can do to separate ourselves from the love of God! He's an awesome God! Especially in His great grace toward us! This is all the more reason why I, for one, know that this was such an amazing grace!

As I thought back on those former teachings, they allowed me to more fully understand the process on the cross. We always refer to Jesus as having died on the cross, but the correct revelation we need here is based on what the scripture says in Galatians 3:13:

> Christ has redeemed us from the curse of the law, having become a curse for us (for it is written, "Cursed is everyone who hangs on a **tree**.")

I shared, in the previous chapters the scripture that tells us the crucifixion took place in an area with a garden nearby. What we now need to think about and get a picture of is Jesus Christ as He is hanging on the tree. Jesus, the second Adam, dies on a tree, and this allows us to follow along a more clear line of thought within the context of the first Adam's sin being the rebellion of touching the tree.

Artists, down through the years, in many of their renderings have depicted Jesus' body with just a couple of trickles of blood here and there, and a few trickles running down His face. They also show Him with a very sparkling, bright, white, hardly-stained-at-all loincloth over the genital area. I don't believe this to be a true depiction. From the moment they arrested Him in the garden until He was nailed to the tree, He never had a minute's rest from the Jewish and Roman leaders of the nation. He had been dragged through their "kangaroo court" trials all night long. Don't forget they were fearful He would probably manage to get away, so they were taking no chances in letting Him out of their sight for a second. Once it was day they began to mutilate His physical body. His flesh had been filleted beyond recognition with the scourging weapon. His face and head were severely swollen from the plucked beard (ladies think about our squirming when we pluck one hair from our eyebrow), and the thorns were so sharp they were gouging into his head! His wrists, not hands, had spikes, not nails like we think, driven into them, and also His feet. He was a bloody, bloody mess! He was steadily losing blood, blood, blood, and more blood! So how is it He could end up with a lily-white loincloth on His body? Not possible! This loincloth would have to be drenched, literally soaked with His blood! What was the ultimate humiliation? The answer is not His being crucified. If anything, crucifixion was almost viewed as a badge of honor. What better way to glory in martyrdom? No, the humiliation was the fact that the loincloth was probably not on Him at all when they nailed Him to the tree! This, too, was typical Roman practice. The men were crucified naked! We cannot continue to dress this event up so as to not blush over embarrassing unmentionables or shudder over the sheer horror of it all. This is why the Bible says in Hebrews 12:2:

Looking unto Jesus, the author and finisher of our faith, who for the joy that was set before Him endured the cross, despising the shame, and has sat down at the right hand of the throne of God.

We cannot begin to understand the embarrassment this was to Him. He was to be hung underneath a sign saying,

JESUS OF NAZARETH
KING OF THE JEWS

There was Jesus hanging there, a naked wretched mess. How could this be nothing short of the absolute worst humiliation ever, He was the King of the Jews? A King being presented in this fashion? Hanging there with His penis exposed in the presence of His own mother, who is standing beneath the cross looking up at her firstborn, her dear son. Now men, I ask you, how many of you could fathom the idea of having your mom see you totally nude as a grown man? No way! The scripture says despising the shame, despising the shame, despising the shame! On top of this shameful process He has to endure, He is still being the obedient Son of God that He always was and also His mother's good Jewish boy. (It was customary in Jewish Law that when there was a deceased husband/father, the son would look after his widowed mother). So even in His dying moments He is seeing to the care of His mom when He commends John to look after her. Even though Jesus is taking care of this business because He loved His mother, it had to be utterly humiliating for Him as a grown man to have to look into the eyes of His mother, His siblings, and His disciples as He hung there nude.

Let's venture back again. Remember, we established earlier that for every act of unrighteousness committed, there had to be an act of righteousness equal to or greater than and contrary to the act of sin done, in order to cancel its authority. We know, according to scripture, that Adam and Eve were naked and not ashamed in Genesis 2:25 before they sinned. According to Genesis 3:7,9 once they committed the sexual sin, however, we can readily see the shame factor had entered in. As much as Jesus hates this situation, He endures the whole despicable thing, because He saw the JOY afar off! He championed our cause and defeated that demon of "shame!" Their nudity was a sin. His nudity was an act of righteousness to counter.

Now here is the final piece to this puzzle. We have now established that Jesus was put through an exhausting trial period without sleep. He has been unmercifully beaten beyond recognition and He is an absolutely bloody mess. He is hanging before all Israel totally nude and humiliated, but He is most certainly the conquering Savior and Bridegroom.

My Parable

Now let's scale this down to a level we can all understand. A man comes home from a hard day at work. He is tired and worn out. He plops down in his comfortable easy chair so he can go through the mail. He somehow finally musters up enough strength to get out of the chair and head for the shower, and when he is done he collapses into bed. His wife has been in the kitchen trying to finish preparing his favorite supper. She wants to be sure to serve it nice and hot. He is finally aroused from his sleep as she brings his supper into the bedroom on a tray. He awakens to eat and passes out again as soon as he is finished with his meal. His wife comes to retrieve the tray and goes to the kitchen to clean and put everything away. She comes back into the bedroom with the thought that her husband will not awaken until it is time to get up and go to work the next morning. Much to her surprise, however, as soon as she undresses her husband happens to awaken and catches a peek of the silhouette of his wife's lovely body. He gets energy from God only knows where! The wife doesn't understand, for the life of her, where he could possibly get the energy needed to make love to her, and to make love to her satisfaction. Yet, she has no intentions of complaining or saying a word, because she's also too happy and satisfied. They make beautiful love. The husband brings his wife such pleasure she has more than a satisfying orgasm, and when he knows she's pleased he proceeds to have his climax. He is so excited and so highly stimulated that he gives out a strong exclamatory remark. He is almost shouting out loud. This signals to the wife that he too has had his climax, and that makes her very happy. The husband is very exhausted and extremely thirsty now. He reaches for his glass of water that he kept on the nightstand after dinner was over. He takes a long cool drink. He fluffs his pillow, reaches over and pulls his adoring wife into his arms and whispers to her, "I love you so much." She looks into his eyes as she kisses his cheek and says, "Honey, I love you, too." Now that they are both satisfied they drift off to sleep. The End.

THE DYING BRIDEGROOM is about to consummate His union with His Bride. This moment is about Jesus Christ, the Bridegroom and The Church, His Bride. Jesus Christ is carrying out spiritually, what married couples do naturally. This, Our Lord's wedding day, has been in the planning stages all of His life. As He hangs on Calvary He is giving of Himself totally and completely for His Bride. Even though He is a horrible sight as He hangs there He is Holy from the crown of His head to the soles of His feet. His entire spirit, soul and body is blameless and pure as He hangs there for you and for me. He is more than willing on this, His wedding day, to die for His Beloved. In a natural marriage, when consummation takes place, there is a great likelihood of a resulting pregnancy. Jesus Christ was most certainly excited as the greatest of all spiritual encounters was coming to completion. Jesus knew His wife, The Church, was going to become pregnant as a result of their love and He was ecstatic! Wait! What do we hear? A shout, a rallying cry! What in the world does He have to shout about? He lets out a shout of triumph before His Heavenly Father and the entire nation of Israel, as they gaze at in Him in shock and disbelief! What does someone do? They run and get Him something to quench His thirst. Why? It was the long awaited climactic end to the deliverance with which He wanted to satisfy His bride. As He cried out in triumph, little did anyone know He thrusted through the "spiritual hymen tissue" of the Bride and it ripped right down the middle. Hymen Tissue? Yes, the hymen tissue was just a few miles away from Calvary. It was the temple veil that hung across the Holy of Holies, blocking our access to the Father! Bang! Two hundred pounds of fabric hits the floor of the Temple and spiritual seed from Jesus Christ is released into the Bride, The

Church. Whoosh! (Matthew 27:51) With this major breakthrough, the sin factor that had originally destroyed all the spiritual sperm in Adam's loins was countered by a catapulting into the spirit of the spiritual sperm of righteousness that cleansed all the seed forever, that is as long as it comes through His precious blood!

This reminds me of an old, beloved hymn I sang for years growing up in the Baptist church. The first few words say:

"There is a fountain, filled with blood, drawn from Emanuel's veins; and sinners plunged beneath that flood, lose all their guilty stains . . . The dying thief rejoiced to see that fountain in his day; and there may I, though vile as he, wash all my sins away."[1]

She, the Bride of Christ, the Church; immediately becomes pregnant with spiritual seed. This is certainly unlike any pregnancy we women have ever known. Now this pregnancy is different for two reasons:

This spiritual bride was only pregnant for fifty-three days. The first babies She birthed was on the day of Pentecost. She had multiple births. She had over three thousand babies at once!

And in those days Peter stood up in the midst of the disciples (altogether the number of names was about a hundred and twenty), Acts 1:15

Then those who gladly received his word were baptized; and that day about three thousand souls were added to them. Acts 2:41

She never has to have another experience to get pregnant again. That one major encounter has rendered her pregnant from that day to this. Over two thousand years later, She is still having babies every hour on the hour all over the world!

Do not marvel that I said to you, 'You must be born again.'
John 3:7

Well, I'm telling you the earth got so excited over the climax it had just experienced, it moved . . . in the form of an earthquake, lightenings, and thunderings. The entire earth became dark as our sweet expended Savior and Bridegroom whispered in the ear of His Father and His Bride with one last exhausted breath, "IT IS FINISHED!"

That was absolutely the best way He knew to express His love. I think He expressed it very well, don't you? He was so tired from the experience that He fell asleep for a solid 72 hours! Matthew 12:40:

> For as Jonah was three days and three nights in the belly of the great fish, so will the Son of Man be three days and three nights in the heart of the earth.

What a rest He needed! Oh . . . how I love Jesus, because He first loved me!

Just as we shared earlier in the book, with God all covenants are ratified by the shedding of blood. Therefore, in the Jewish law, with regard to a natural union, it was customary to present proof of the purity of the virgin bride. Jesus did likewise, because He said He came to fulfill the law, not destroy it, so He, too, showed proof of the purity of His Bride. In this case, unlike a natural union, Jesus, Himself, was responsible for Her purity. Now, in a natural union, according to Orthodox Jewish custom, this is done by having the Bride place a clean white cloth beneath her body during the consummation act, and if she is indeed a virgin, the blood from the rupture of the hymen tissue will run onto the cloth. This cloth is then presented to the parents for their inspection. When the parents are done with their inspection and conclude everything seems to be in order, and the bride is worthy of their son, the bridegroom, then the wedding celebration really kicks off into high gear! Jesus did the same. We read in Hebrews 9:11-14:

> But Christ came as High Priest of the good things to come, with the greater and more perfect tabernacle not made with

hands, that is, not of this creation. Not with the blood of goats and calves, but with His own blood He entered the Most Holy Place once for all, having obtained eternal redemption. For if the blood of bulls and goats and the ashes of a heifer, sprinkling the unclean, sanctifies for the purifying of the flesh, how much more shall the blood of Christ, who through the eternal Spirit offered Himself without spot to God, cleanse your conscience from dead works to serve the living God?

In that Jesus Christ truly loved His Bride, there was nothing He would not have done to bring Her back into a right relationship with His Father. He, therefore, did not just talk about His great love for Her, He proved it by His death. Hence this is the uncovering of yet another mystery and we now understand what Paul was saying to the church of the Ephesians. In chapter 5:25-32:

Husbands, love your wives, just as Christ also loved the church and gave Himself for her, that He might sanctify and cleanse her with the washing of water by the word, that He might present her to Himself a glorious church, not having spot or wrinkle or any such thing, but that she should be holy and without blemish. So husbands ought to love their own wives as their own bodies; he who loves his wife loves himself. For no one ever hated his own flesh, but nourishes and cherishes it, just as the Lord does the church. For we are members of His body, of His flesh and of His bones. "For this reason a man shall leave his father and mother and be joined to his wife, and the two shall become one flesh." This is a great mystery, but I speak concerning Christ and the church.

The end of this book, but I pray the beginning of a transformed life in HIM. I'll see you, when I see you . . .

—Pastor B

Notes

It Feels Good Not To Know

1. Essenes quoted from, *Unger's Bible Dictionary*, see Bibliography. "Although the Bible never mentions the Essenes, they are described by several ancient historians. The Essenes are an important part of the background to the New Testament, showing the beliefs and practices of one Jewish religious group at the time of John the Baptist and Jesus. People have been especially interested in the Essenes since the discovery of the Dead Sea Scrolls at Qumran. The people who lived at Qumran probably were a group of Essenes." (*Nelson's Illustrated Bible Dictionary*, see bibliography.)

A Dialogue On The Issue Of Masturbation

A discussion with Kim-Andréa Belle Richardson.

My Parable

1. *There is a Fountain Filled with Blood*, by Lowell Mason and Wm. Cowper. See Bibliography.

Bibliography

Biblesoft's New Exhaustive Strong's Numbers and Concordance with Expanded Greek-Hebrew Dictionary. Seattle, Washington:Biblesoft and International Bible Translators, Inc., 1994.

Lamsa, George M. *The Holy Bible From Ancient Eastern Manuscripts: Containing the Old and New Testament Translated from the Peshitta, The Authorized Bible of the Church of the East.* Philadelphia, Pennsylvania: A.J. Holman Company, 1957.

Merriam-Webster's Collegiate Dictionary, Tenth Edition. Springfield, Massachusetts: Merriam-Webster.

Nelson's Illustrated Bible Dictionary. Nashville, Tennessee: Thomas Nelson Publishers, 1986.

Sing Unto the Lord. Hazelwood, Missouri: Word Aflame Press, 1978.

The New Complete Works of Josephus, Revised and Expanded Edition. Translated by William Whiston. Grand Rapids, Michigan: Kregel Publications, 1999.

The New Unger's Bible Dictionary. Chicago, Illinois: Moody Press, 1988.

The Works of Philo: New Updated Edition. Translated by C. D. Yonge. Hendrickson Publishers, Inc., 1993.

Today's English Version, Second Edition. New York, New York: American Bible Society, 1992.

Worley, Win. *Conquering the Hosts of Hell.* Lansing, Illinois: H.B.C., 1991. See also WRW Publications, Highland, IN.

Scripture Index

About the Author

PASTOR BARBARA WALLACE ERKINS is cofounder and Senior Pastor of The Eagles' Vision Christian Center in Cleveland, Ohio. Ordained in ministry in 1992, Pastor Barbara has taught the Word for many years. As a dynamic, passionate, and often humorous teacher, she imparts truth and revelation to the Body of Christ. Pastor Barbara understands human passions and ministers freedom and hope to singles and married couples.

She and her husband, Pastor Jesse, have been married for nearly 25 years and have two grown children.

Praise for
By Any Other Name It's Still Sex

"Seemingly bizarre, but at it's best compelling! A **must read** for those who dare to move beyond the surface and into the deeper things of God."

Rev. Dianne Lewis Brown,
President, Vision Planning Services, Inc.

"A courageous exploration of a difficult topic. Barbara Erkins provides compelling reasons and practical ideas for embracing the gift of our sexuality in a God-centered way."

M.M.,
Survivor of Clergy Sexual Abuse

By Any Other Name It's Still Sex provides an understanding of the nature of sex according to God. Pastor B has done a masterful job of contemporarily explaining societal sex issues through biblical teachings. Every prospective parent, parent and teen should read this book and share its wisdom.

Camille Bridges, MBA,
National Alliance of Market Developers,
Cleveland Chapter President

I have been spiritually uplifted and given a new dimension in my medical practice as a gynecologist. In this sordidly complex world, Pastor Barbara, through her travels in life, has managed to take the scriptures and tie it into what we have come to know medically. This is a must read for the understanding of the parent and young adult.

J.M. Erkins, MD, FAOG, MBA,
Chief & Director of OB/GYN &
Women and Children Services,
Cleveland Clinic Foundation,
Huron Road Medical Center &
Medical Director, Feminine Health Concerns

"I will never be the same. I now know the truth and I have been set free. Pastor B shares profound scriptural insight and its about time we take time to know the truth about sex. Your life and our children's lives depend on it."

Minister Tammy Hoogstad,
CKB Angel Ministries

Additional copies of this book and other book titles
from Dawn Treader Publications are
available at your local bookstore or directly
from the Publisher.

Dawn Treader Publications
A ministry of Morning Star And Company, Inc.
P.O. Box 22175
Beachwood, OH 44122

www. dawntreaderpublications.com
www. morningstarandcompany.org

Pastor Barbara Wallace Erkins
ministers the Word through seminars,
conferences, and special events.

For more information contact
Barbara Erkins Ministries (BEM)
PO Box 221165
Beachwood, Ohio 44122

Colophon

Set in Bell MT and Brickham Script
Bell is a trademark of The Monotype Corporation
Brickham Script is a trademark of Adobe Systems Incorporated

Layout and Design by KAR at Studio Downstairs, Inc.
Special thanks to Editor-in-Chief, Annie S. Thomas
Apple Paintings by Nicora Gangi
Author Photograph by Bill Beck
Imprint Design by Alexandra Harris
Printed and Bound in the United States of America
Special Thanks to Kathy King and Jan Stevens
at Sheridan Books, Inc.